MUMMYJIHAD

ESSENTIAL POETS SERIES 273

**Canada Council   Conseil des Arts
for the Arts   du Canada**

**ONTARIO ARTS COUNCIL
CONSEIL DES ARTS DE L'ONTARIO**

an Ontario government agency
un organisme du gouvernement de l'Ont

Canadä

Guernica Editions Inc. acknowledges the support of the Canada Council
for the Arts and the Ontario Arts Council. The Ontario Arts Council
is an agency of the Government of Ontario.

We acknowledge the financial support of the Government of Canada.

EARL FOWLER

MUMMYJIHAD

GUERNICA
EDITIONS

TORONTO – CHICAGO – BUFFALO – LANCASTER (U.K.)
2020

Michael Mirolla, editor
Cover and interior design: Errol F. Richardson
Guernica Editions Inc.
287 Templemead Drive, Hamilton (ON), Canada L8W 2W4
2250 Military Road, Tonawanda, N.Y. 14150-6000 U.S.A.
www.guernicaeditions.com

Distributors:
Independent Publishers Group (IPG)
600 North Pulaski Road, Chicago IL 60624
University of Toronto Press Distribution,
5201 Dufferin Street, Toronto (ON), Canada M3H 5T8
Gazelle Book Services, White Cross Mills
High Town, Lancaster LA1 4XS U.K.

First edition.
Printed in Canada.

Legal Deposit – First Quarter
Library of Congress Catalog Card Number: 2019947050
Library and Archives Canada Cataloguing in Publication
Title: Mummyjihad / Earl Fowler.
Other titles: Mummy jihad
Names: Fowler, Earl, author.
Series: Essential poets ; 273.
Description: Series statement: Essential poets series ; 273 | Poems.
Identifiers: Canadiana 20190158204 | ISBN 9781771835084 (softcover)
Classification: LCC PS8611.O87685 M86 2020 | DDC C811/.6—dc23

Contents

In the jewel in the lotus   11

I sleep but am awakened   13

One person in a room   15

Harlequinade   16

Dégringolade   18

Suffering alone exists, none who suffer   21

Incurious seeker   22

The sign says: TODAY IS WEDNESDAY   24

Through India Gate   26

What this story lacks   28

Life is a burning house, my friend. Come to the shadow play   29

Not to go on all-fours, that is the law   31

Have you tried the morgue? They're open all night   33

The Dirt Age   35

All the textbooks scant the lives of women   37

Lapidarium   38

The universe should not exist, CERN study confirms   39

In the fourth stage of dhyana, all sensations, even of happiness
       and unhappiness, of joy and sorrow, disappear   41

Ask me obliquely, as you think befits a personage of my stature,
       where I am from   43

Oh, just, subtle, and mighty Buckley's Formula!   45

An unreal world constantly presses upon mine   47

Performance art in assisted living   49

Fitbit America   51

Automatic reply   53

Homo faber   55

Explaining the plot line of Hindi soap opera   56

One of destiny's many pranks   57

Piya Chattopadhyay and all these Indian girls on the news now   59

LinkedOut updates   60

It's Slinky, it's Slinky, it's fun for a girl and a boy   62

I don't know what God's wish is   64

Consult women and do the opposite   65

Fairy chimneys   66

Rambling randonnée through the halls of Happydale   67

In my heart I kept saying: Let it be now, let it be now   68

'Cause if you get too close, you know I'm gone like a cool breeze   70

Sleep is my lover among The Dead   71

Ars amatoria   73

I got fingers on my blisters   74

I might be some sort of intermediate stage   75

May contain explicit violence, frequent coarse language, sexual

       activity and/or horror   77

Broadway melody of 1984   78

Hail, city of timbits, faint red roofs of mouths   80

The laugh riot of two continents   81

Hook and loop   82

Shuffling from point A to point B   83

Battleship Potemkin   84

Part II, chapter IX   85

Who I am, what I was, has been detonated all to Allahu Akbar

       in a handbasket   87

Madam Z has corrupted Brother 12   88

A bitumen than I am, Ganja Din   89

I started to read the 7 Habits of Highly Effective People   91

Seven habits of highly ineffective people   92

Night work ahead. Please slow down.   94

Come with the holy fires   95

Will the dead, like the old in these places, have nothing to say?   96

How often have I lain beneath rain on a strange roof, thinking

       of home   97

Femunculus   98

Dishes fly   99

I am a garment of light from the first second   100

Tell me what to do   102

Ghostly assignations at the lower nodal point   103

EAT ME   104

I don't want to   106

Feng shui for constipation   107

Where there is nothing, there is God   109

All this foofaraw around Abrahamic, monotheistic religions   110

Address to bones with wedding rings mixed up in the dust and the gold stoppings of innumerable decayed teeth at La Grande Galerie of the Muséum national d'histoire naturelle   111

You can hold the skull of Descartes   113

Well, what did I expect?   114

Mindfulness, and right concentration   116

There is a thing confusedly formed   117

We walk on air, Watson. Make notes.   119

Saturday night's all right for sewing   121

Where are my little purses with the coloured flowers?   123

Betwixt plinth and lintel   124

A life full of incident and romance   125

From the portal of submission, everything happens slowly   127

Club des diagrammes de Venn   129

Acedia   131

Crepuscular clutter   133

Beldam in Bedlam   135

Impossible to feign   137

Practise your beauty, blue girls, before it fail   139

Lascaux   140

Does your family know your wishes, Mrs. Singh?   142

Sunday mornin' my head is bad   144

Take Mummy out to the sidewalk   145

Statement of orthodox faith in opposition to certain heresies 147

Graphomania 148

The cenobitic life 150

Bedroom community 152

Ian Hanomansing is looking so sad 153

I am in the background of somebody's snapshot of something 154

This person cannot be reached 156

A rendezvous is missed and the author sheds her tears at Grand
      Central Station 157

Paradise by The Weather Network screen 158

We are sequestered and mournful junkie ghosts in far-flung
      pharmaceutical hazes 160

What's it like to be an old bat? 161

Sylvia, who are you? 162

Non compos mentis in the sangha of the dead 164

Why yes, I would like a bag 166

Address to the five ascetics in the deer park at Saanich 167

En déshabillé 168

Between the clock and the bed 169

Progression d'effet 170

Missed call 172

A place for mom 173

Even my nose has changed 175

Noctilucence 176

Curtains 178

Bocca Baciata 180

I need a better reason to be here than Butter Rum Life Savers 182

Ragtime 183

Boats from the underground 188

Acknowledgements 192

About the Author 193

In the jewel in the lotus

Out of dark water,
I arise on a golden-centred,
many-petalled lotus.
Carve myself
from Persian consonants of sleep.
Wherever I step, a lily springs up.
Om mani padme hum.

I am losing the ability to discern the difference
between the transitory and the permanent.
I am hesitant about the distinction
between inside and outside,
the me and the not-me,
the boundaries of self.
Yakshi and stupa appear together,
aspects of the same sacred complex.

I am the stoker and the stoked.
A crockpot of decorticated Christ consciousness.
A kind of erasure of personality.
Formidable erosions of contour, at any rate.
Dehors-texte. Dehors-mezzotint.
A liminal thing at some kind of threshold.
First-time cosmic smudge, long-time listener.
The crinkled gold foil of modernism.
A coat of all the skins of all the creatures in all the world.

A game of existential Whack-A-Mole.
The song the porter sings.
A kind of insubstantial territory.
What the wind seeks when it goes out alone.

Trees make obeisance. Fronds litter the road.
Flowers spill from my lips as the wind overtakes me.
Oh, what quenchless feud is this?
The Holy Mother vacuums under my feet.

For 40 years, I have kept my beautiful hair
under an astonishing assortment of shower caps.
How easily an untended garden returns to wilderness.

An accident of serotonin, perhaps.

Tutte tutte, vutte vutte, patte patte, katte katte

It's still rocking chair to me.

I sleep but am awakened

Open my eyes, behold! the horrid thing stands at my chair side,
opening the curtains and looking at me with yellow, watery, speculative eyes.
He is turning off the smoke detector, which has been buzzing for an hour
but which only frightens me and to which, in any case,
I don't know how to respond.

Maybe it is the ghost of Daddy.
Daddy who used to sing, "I'll be Ram for Christmas. You can tandoori."
Thought it was hilarious.

Probably it is the printer only.
He is married to Rekha.
A stupid-looking, slack-mouthed fellow.
Skimpole.

This printer stepped out of a Caravaggio canvas, mandolin in tow.
Dripping mysterious pigments.
He uses words to cover the sleeper, not to wake her.
He took photos of my diplomas from Agra and Nagpur
and I was flattered until he also took photos
of their club sandwiches at White Spot.

No, I can't feel at home in this world anymore.
I am depressurized as Oddjob.
Magnum P.I., I urgently request your gun-toting assistance.

People with green eyes are pagli.

I live in the intense inane.
Who will I be if I stay?
I ought to jump overboard like Virginia Woolf.
Like Natalie Wood.
Like the third wife of William Shatner.
Whatever her name was.
To be something that lies under the sun and feels it.

There is no possible way that Aishwarya Rai has blue-green eyes,
whatever Rekha insists and whatever the computer says.
They are blue only.

Like Andromeda, chained to the shore.
Brünnhilde, stranded on that rock.
Surrounded by fire.
I'll have what she's having.

One person in a room

The curtain goes up on the stage,
and I see it as a very potent question:
What is going to happen to the one person in a room?
Is someone going to open the door and come in?
Good God! How long can she possibly sit like that?

The room is a speck of warmth and light in the darkness.
It is a precarious foothold.
Here all the mystery of creation
becomes threadbare mystification.
Last day: Air Canada seat sale.

Time moves slower downstairs.
Gravity and acceleration are indistinguishable.
Einstein proved that much.

I travel at a rate of one second per second.

I signed a form, you see, giving them permission.
Meals are prepared, my tablets are delivered
and baths are dispensed on Sundays.

The more acute the experience,
the less articulate its expression.
It's all hammering and sawing in the distance.
I sit in a chair by the bed.

Harlequinade

The old men in this place all rub their heads like Stan Laurel.
The women have gingerbread hearts on their breasts.
Pantomimes of the Funambules.

Here we are now. Entertain us.
Bus outings to the mall and the casino.
Lovely patios, gardens and courtyards, parking, lockers,
beauty salon, sample menus, motorized wheelchairs with flags.
I feel stupid. They're contagious. A mulatto. An albino.

I am not prejudiced against the Chinese,
but there was a Chinaman in my village who sold kimonos
and you should have heard what the children called him.

See, that is why I was concerned only
when it looked like my granddaughter might have Chinese eyes.

Also appearing: Sammy White as Gus.

They say no cosmic wormholes have been detected.
But come see the cubbyhole I have carved
with the cardboard consciousness that remains
on a mote of dust
suspended in a sunbeam
at the bottom of the stairs.

Lady Bertram did not think deeply.

The Germans wore grey.
You wore blue.
Here is my voice already fixed with night.
I have been taught by masters.

Help of the helpless, oh.

There was an old lady whose folly
induced her to sit in a holly;
Whereon by a thorn her pants being torn
She swore in a Bengali volley.

Dégringolade

My own enzymes are digesting me at 98.6 F to beat hell.
Me! Miss Polypeptide Chain of 1947!
I am breaking down proteins at an astronomical rate.

A sort of solvent meditating on the lotus feet of Vishnu,
I have located the substrate of my seeming consciousness.
It is a quasi-quantum effect in the microtubules of the cortex.

I am one of those women who sit at the back,
yawning behind a rice-paper curtain.

My legs, I was told, were my best feature.
Now my stockings hang like Hungarian sausage skins.
My hair looks like it was mussed in the ring
by Whipper Billy Watson, two-time
world heavyweight wrestling champion.

I am enclosed in a supple integument of same-old-story.

People from England who live in Canada
think they can just come into your house
and comment on the floral arrangements
because they think they're still over the Indians.

I am in a grooming line of money-changing monkeys.
A coat on a tick.
I am a billion trillion molecules in a million,
trillion trillion cubic light years.

A flower, and yet not a flower;
of mist, and yet not of mist.
Gusts of particle exchange in a gravity sink.

My mother was a Jew and that's why I can't eat that.
Whatever Rekha has cooked.
What is this?

I began in a state of infinite density and no size.
Infinite possibility divided by the square root
of cooked cabbage and sweet Francis Ann.

I know who I am, and who I may be, if I choose.
I am the footprint of the All.
I am a manifestation of Brahma in the field of time.

This, by the way, is a fabulous honour.

The DNA in my body, unsnarled,
would stretch to the sun and back.
I am a god hidden from myself.
I must have had a good reason.

I am some sort of a machine
built by a message
to perpetuate that message.
And I still can't remember who you are
or why you've come into my room.

I always go into the bathroom and close the door
and hide in the tub when there is loud thunder
and I am alone.

Stop the presses. I want to get off.

Simply the thing I am shall make me live.
There's place and means for every woman alive.
I'll after them.

I have opened my mouth unto the Lord.
I cannot go back.
But Dr. Chandra, will I dream?

Suffering alone exists, none who suffer

The deed there is, but no doer thereof.
Nirvana is, but no one seeking it.
Path there is, but none who travel it.
Hot in Cleveland is on, but I can't be bothered.

Incurious seeker

I am the ghost on the wrong side of the vacuum tube.
Rita Hayworth eternally teasing off her gloves in *Gilda*.
Love lockets go straight through my hands.
Put the blame on Mame, boys.

And then the ultimate mood killer:
"Mummy. Did you go kaka today?"
Arrey? Did somebody turn up the gravity in here?

Retrovistas of loss and betrayal.
My hair grown into leaves.
Arms into branches.
Feet held fast by sluggish roots.

Turn around, bright eyes.
She of the Ointment Jar reconsiders wary affiliations.

I think I'll take an After Eight mint chocolate thin.
Or maybe a Halls Mentho-Lyptus.

And then I am the young Audrey Hepburn,
performing a bohemian dance at a Parisian nightclub.
Meena Kumari or Geeta Bali mouthing words and spinning in 1953.
I am in the arms of Shammi Kapoor.
Life pays me off the books.

When it comes to Hindi, south Indians are like Quebecers and English.
They know how to speak it but they won't.
The French don't know how to make pancakes.

Every now and then I get a little bit lonely
with the tired, aching legs
of Billie Jean King.

The sign says: TODAY IS WEDNESDAY

As if that has a vestige of significance to anyone here.
Where we were going has become where we are.
Who we are can no longer be who we were.

We are refugees from a future that never arrived.
What we set out to do is a spent Brillo pad in a drained sink.
The same dull round, even of a universe.

Moments. Ah, moments. My moments.
The dog's moments.

On the aglet-frazzled, sibilating sneakers of eternity,
we wander the back forty of *Bulfinch's Mythology*
as half-human satyrs and harpies, griffins, centaurs
and 21 perfectly timed dirty photos you'll never forget.
(Sonam Kapoor goes braless for *Vogue India* shoot.)

We seen pretty people disappear like smoke.
Do they take 'em for espresso?
Yeah, I guess so. I wish I knew.

We're the moonbeams who didn't get out of the jar.
Moonlight and love songs, forever out of date.
The others are waiting for me in Arts and Crafts.

Fabulous birds and Nereids and so forth.
Baba Yoga casts spells in the basement.
We are the signatories to the Pact of Forgetting
in the Valley of the Inchoate.

The Steadicam tracks me in single-take shots
of unusual duration
by the rivers of Babylon.
By Grand Central Station, I sat down and slept.

Hrithik Roshan has two thumbs on his right hand
but this they always hide.
Throw my ticket out the window.

Three thumbs up.

I don't know whether I'm in a garden
or on some kind of crowded avenue.
I can't even remember what it is
I came here to get away from.

Through India Gate

A hundred roots drink silently
at this Husky House truck stop of the soul.
Carry your toothbrush and a facecloth
during an aimless meander along the hallway.
Iggle Piggle is having a rest in Upsy Daisy's bed.

There's nothing you can do
but you can learn how to be us in time.
It's easy. Who wants cake and ice cream?

Laugh, kookaburra. Laugh, kookaburra.
Give me to drink mandragora
that I might sleep out the great ghat of time.

I sit here without moving.
But under me, all moves.
And moves me gently up and down
and from side to side.
Past midnight.
Never knew such silence.
The Earth might be uninhabited.

Waking fakirs and stall-holders put out their wares.
Orange garlands, costume jewellery, brass pots and joss sticks.
Watering cans slump from taps in all the cemeteries in all the world.

On the riverbank, the saris have been laid out to dry,
fluttering empty sleeves like the sea.
Bring me some Marcelle face wash.

I am firmly in the not here, not now.
A courtesan in a woodblock print.
There's a front seat and a back seat
and a window in between.

My Antony is away.
There is a scratch on my thigh.
Picking gooseberries, no point in going on.

And Beta, I have to go to the bathroom.
You don't have Marcelle face wash?

What this story lacks

Deft impersonations of 19th-century prose, a printer wearing a sweet-smelling pomade, Dr. Ridley's Pungent Pills for the Treatment of Female Irregularities, a trip to the morgue to identify the body, a lick of originality, the journey of Abraham from the Mesopotamian city of Ur to Canaan's sere and rocky landscape two thousand years before Christ, a scarred villain, an opium den, the people in the cheap seats clapping, coyness about zesty sw--ring, a pair of reunited lost siblings, an inappropriate smile like a rictus reflecting from an old woman's TV screen, florid accounts of ecstasies, suitcases stuffed with body parts, Daddy's hideous, smoked-glass lamp shaped like a panther, a woodpecker toothpick dispenser that once belonged to my Uncle Keith (similar examples of which are now worth an astounding $85 US on eBay), a wicker birdcage given as a wedding present, Turkish slippers and a fringed skirt, a reason for being, a beribboned tambourine, a heretofore secret cache of passionate letters from Bruno Gerussi to Al Waxman, a consumptive wife in the attic, the assassination of Anwar Sadat, reproductions of great masterpieces given away with Babbitt's soap, one improbable coincidence after another, hand-rolled cigarettes and clandestine smoking in the garden by a man who drives a Renault, the repositioning of a mat and bucket after a squalid masturbation scene, sponsored content, foreseeable catastrophic turns and dilettantish contemplation of jumping from the Tallahatchie Bridge until, at last, in one opportune plot turn ... no, sorry, it's time for *McMillan & Wife* on MeTV. Someday I'll write it all down on hoarded butcher paper. If I'm curt, then I apologize. But today it's liver and onions and quality viewing. The cost of things not covered by most provincial health care plans keeps going up. Maybe the night reporter can make some calls.

Life is a burning house, my friend. Come to the shadow play

And so I have come home
to a ridiculous fantasy
that this is a home.

Like the returning Ulysses,
I cannot prove I am who I say I am.

I brought two pairs of panties only.
And I forgot my oils because they were rushing me.
But I brought stamps.

(The excuse I gave for weeks for avoiding all social interaction at home
was that I was packing for this trip.)

Throw my suitcase out there, too.

I am a shade in a half-aware dance
powered by electro-chemical tumult:
the machine in the ghost: Deus absconditus.

The snake with three green leaves in its mouth.
I wander all night in my vision.

The illusion of self has slipped through
the hole in my bucket, dear Liza,
onto a fun house of moving floors,
rotating barrels, sudden updrafts
and belated refractions

out of the cradle endlessly rocking
of what I thought I was
and then it is time for breakfast
and they bring me my tablets
and take off my sock
and phew, for a minute there

Not to go on all-fours, that is the law

They look up each day as I arrive for lunch.
Grim, ungainly, ghastly, gaunt
ominous birds of yore
perched on the shoulder of the skeleton
standing on the black sun
dragging, dirge-like behind it,
fetters of bog and mist and wedgies of toilet paper.

This is what God has willed for me.
My skin bruises, chafes and splits easily now
as if I were some kind of inedible fruit
suffused with my own mystery,
constricted by the trailing grave clothes
and occasional bladder leaks.

I am a spirit of some all-too-common rate
followed by the pound sign.
I see the world in a grain of sand
and in that sand the men do stand
inert and expressionless,
phenomenological geckos
with visas to nowhere
tucked into the pockets
of this interminable last Sabbath.

Someone should invent a room where dogs
could go to the bathroom only,
so they wouldn't have to go outside.

Yet even now in this harrowing of hell,
I am watched lustily through glass doors
by camphorous old men
perched on the shoulder of the skeleton
that stands on the black sun of time
— Peaseblossom! Cobweb! Moth! And Mustard seed! —
spare arrangements of headstone-lichen stubble on sallow flesh,
shaggy-cuffed spindthrifts of saliva and ligament
in electrically charged trousers, hairless legs
limpid as icicles hanging from the hooded moon.

Inhuman contortions from ark to ark.
Grotesque movements.
Strained acrobatical feats.
Byzantine icons. Byzantine icons.
So Fritz Lang!
They've been this way since 1956.

I stand in the dark with drooping eyes by the worst-suffering
and the most restless.
I like thin Cheezies only. Not these thick ones.
I pass my hands soothingly to and fro a few inches from them.
Keep moving boys. I'll see you at the track.

One uses the little blade on his pocketknife to clean his ears.
I imagine we're having minestrone again.

Have you tried the morgue? They're open all night

The way I see it, once you wind up here,
it doesn't matter who you were or what you did.

Whether you ate grass and died in a ditch
in the brown water where dead leaves had rotted.
Stopped eating, sat mute and motionless in a corner
of a small, rented room in an expanding universe,
inert and vaguely sad.

Were nailed like a stoat to the stable door.
In this place, we are all Snow White
living on blind mole's time.
Our purpose nothing but ease.

Raise the palace of Pandemonium.
The night light Rekha made a special trip
to the store for yesterday glows only.
I require one that shines.

The world has devoured the grandmother.
It lies in her bed.
How frightened I have been.
How dark it is inside the world.

Even George Raft couldn't piece this one together.
I am unacknowledged, certainly, but in this place,
I am not even the legislator of my own bowels.
I abhor myself.

Today I DustBustered a paperclip.
It seemed like enough.

That's the 20th century for you.
Automobiles. Chauffeurs. Chauffeurs' daughters.

These Hindi channels are running out of shows.
I walk in beauty, like the night.

The Dirt Age

Tessellated clay comes up through the cracks in my floorboards.
I am travelling second-class in Galicia and picking up crab lice.
I hear the slow soughing and sighing glissandi of roots.
I am pregnant with the globe of the Earth.

I am wearing stockings fried as Ethel Rosenberg's.
Her hands lying on the quilt like two of them roots dug up.
I am self-taut, under a ceiling of descending grubs.
Droplets hang in the air but cannot fall.

The little waves, with their soft, white hands
efface the footprints in the sands.
Ply stemming nightly toward the pole.
Each step more poignantly oracular.

We are edged with mist.
A blue, uncertain, stumbling buzz.
A ritual dance around a centre.
We live off the smell of offerings.

Cage-brassiered Salomé the temptress remembers
every lack of nerve, every failure of will
with Theda Bara eyes like the eyelids of the morning.

Even the Hindu girls now wear these …
(pained look of unfathomable disdain)
clothes … that show everything.

Is it the motion of the sea
that makes drowned Ceyx raise his head?
Warily, sportsman!
Though I lie so sleepy and sluggish,
the tap of my flukes is death.
The lost traveller's dream under the hill.

Paradise is behind me now.
Click here to see mind-blowing side boobs on Doug Ford.

All the textbooks scant the lives of women

Who eat Cheezies from cellophane bags and watch TV.
Who mysteriously become flesh in the laughing air,
bringing together what is fragment and riddle and dreadful chance.

Who leave empty Halls Mentho-Lyptus wrappers discreetly under pews.
Who are not infrequently remarked upon for their "colourful clothing."
Who might as well have spoons dangling from their foreheads
like Russia's mystical, magnetic women, ticking time.
Cloche. Sonnez là. Cloche. Sonnez là.

I never have problems going to the bathroom.
Only here.
Womb of some ancient earth-mother cult.

That's right, I'm not from Texas.
Go ahead and complain ruefully in piquant letters to the editor
about the obdurate failure of the immigrant to integrate.
Ban turbans and head scarves for the sake of social cohesion.

The white TV president is angry about strong black men kneeling.
Isn't that what he wanted all along?

Badhiya, badhiya, that's all folks.

Lapidarium

Whose tombstone is the moonstone,
with its crabbed inscriptions
crumbling on lozenge rills?

The moonstone is our tombstone.
Skullcap to the cosmos.
Death mask of the Earth.

The universe should not exist, CERN study confirms

I could have told them that.
It's all gone a bit upside-down moth in windowsill.
Less rapture in blue, eternally expanding and contracting,
than recurring motif of bloating and abdominal pain.

Your towels are too heavy.

When the twilight is gone, when no songbirds are singing,
fire a T-shirt cannon into the crowd for figuring that one out,
you big dummies. What do I care anyway?

I am from the Sunday school.
I sing soprano in the upstairs choir.
I get unlimited calls to almost 60 countries, including India.

Your pillows are too hard.

I am the Kardashians of sleep.
Eurydice never needs winding,
never needs winding, never needs.

I drew a map of Canada.
The executioner has cut off my feet
to make me stop dancing.
O Canada.

Caught in a lie or a self-contradiction,
remember that a good cough
always trumps the most rational argument
of one's adversary.

Your pillows are too soft.

Dr. Venkman, you've come all this way.
Would you like to check the refrigerator?

My prayer is to linger with you
at the end of the day
in a dream that's divine.
This little light of mine.
When you're strange,
faces come out of the rain.

I'm going to let them shine.
I spent my 90th birthday alone in a nursing home.
And papa would've shot them
if he knew what they'd done.

In the fourth stage of dhyana, all sensations, even of happiness and unhappiness, of joy and sorrow, disappear

Only equanimity and awareness remain.
The grip of the sloth is so strong
that sometimes they are found still clinging to branches,
months after dying.
Moths have been found
feeding on the algae
that grows along the deep groove
that develops along the midriff.

Of course I'll hold for the next available
customer service representative.

The yogini, too, can turn her head 270 degrees
without leaving her chair.
She was once a voluptuous being.
There were tales of Tantric rites and practices.
(Sax, two licks to bridge)

Kids! Connect the beards of the Beats on Benzedrine.
Win a prize!

Now her eyes have become endless sandstorms,
lending the forest a feeling of dark and occult power.
Bending with open eyes over the shut eyes of sleepers,
wandering and confused, lost to myself, ill-assorted,
contradictory, pausing, gazing, bending, and stopping.
A great beast's foot is chained.

I need to eat all the time because of my pills.
See, they are connected.
Have you seen my stamps?

But I am seeing the goddess.
I am taking darsán.
She stares back with bulbous, saucer eyes.

Like the beam of a lightless star turning on an axle
whose vibrations I can sense in this chair.
A great beast's foot is chained.

It stamps, and stamps, and stamps.
Like the flap of a wave; the kiss of a wave.
I rock to the conclusion that I am my own other.
The artist is the one with nothing to say.

You're not the only one adrift on this ocean.
I sail a schooner round the Horn to Mexico.
Shake the cosmic dust out of my hair.
Micro-meteorites from the birth of the solar system.

I always know what day it is by the shows.
But here, see, it is different.

My fundamental stance is passivity. After all,
Mrs. Dalloway said she would buy the flowers herself.

Rumpelmayer's men are coming.

Ask me obliquely, as you think befits a personage of my stature, where I am from

When I was a girl in Bluebirds,
we sang *Kookaburra sits in the Old Gum Tree.*
Once, the Maiden Baden Powell came to Damoh to visit us
and she held our hands and we sang for her so nicely.

She looked like an English teacher I remember
who stayed behind after independence.
She gave me kisses under the mosquito net.
Her teeth were out. Mine, too, now.

Yesterday, a woman with the same British accent
asked me if I am enjoying my visit to this country.
I have been here since 1971.

Ask me if I am having a hard time adapting to the winters.
Tell me I am lucky that my skin does not show my age.
That wouldn't be because I have the sense to stay out of the sun.

Also I buy concealer (correction dark spots).
Anti-aging, skin-tone matching, Maybelline mascara.
Firming and lifting L'Oréal time-match, super-blendable,
blush-rose, smart-shade powder texturizes as it moisturizes.
He forgets I am 90.

Merry Maids do not believe I am a grandmother.

Barefoot, I make a threadless way down the strange lanes.
Stepping with light feet,
swiftly and noiselessly stepping and stopping.
How hopeless under ground falls the remorseful day.
Still, they say I can keep my existing phone number.

They say I couldn't be a great-grandmother, I look so young.

Happy weekend, everyone.
I'm off to a social nudism event!

Oh, just, subtle, and mighty Buckley's Formula!

Buckley's is the colour of the sadhus.
Long-haired, celibate and dipped slickly in ochre
after lifetimes of spiritual exercises in Varanasi ghats.

Give me an ounce of civet, good apothecary.
Drown me in all the drowsy syrups of the world.
I'm a quicksilver girl.
A lover of the world.

Everything has become progressively pointillist,
as if I were standing too close to that billboard in Times Square
where a giant GI puffs real smoke rings out of gargantuan Camels.

I drown in the spray of phenomena.
I am woven in with the violets.
If nothing is more real than nothing,
anything is less real than everything.
That's logic for you.
Or maybe it's the other way around.

Every day I am so busy
with all the cooking and washing and sewing
and from 5 to 11:30 is show time.
That is why I never finished packing.

We must not ask "And then?" too often.
Send them all my salary
on the waters of oblivion.

(And now, a brief moment of factitious freedom
sucking peppermints
on the way into the presbytery.)

An unreal world constantly presses upon mine

For example, I just had a conversation with my mother.
I hadn't the heart to tell her she was dead.
She was laughing about the time I played Mary Magdalene
and how one of her saris slowly slipped to my ankles.

She said she and my father had nothing in common.
Except for all the children, of course.

At school, they called Usha "English" because she was light-skinned.
They called Rachel "Jewish."
Me, they called "Bengali" because I looked more like my father.

I don't need to read. I get all my information on TV.
You know my eyes hurt.
I've read all I need to read,
and when I started having babies,
I didn't want to read anymore.

Old Mrs. Wright taught my parents to be Christians
until they could break away from her arms and play deck tennis.
Naked boys sat on buffaloes wading genital-deep in irrigated fields.

Old stancher!
Blow.

But I came here to rest.
To be cleansed of seven demons.
Not to be reminded of these things.
(It'll be just like a hotel, the printer said.)

America lies on a couch in a cell with the TV on.
"Lay your head on my lap," Trump Baby says.
Hardened solipsists always manage to take a wrong turn.
In Brer'merica, I lie low.

My father wants to take me to the morning star again.
To do nothing is the hardest thing of all.

Tie me with fences and drag me down.

(An epilogue in some later editions adds the fate of the dogs and ants.)

Performance art in assisted living

Marina Abramović stares across a table
and museum visitors burst into tears.

A rank amateur.

I stare across a table at no one
and no one bursts into tears.

The back seat has left a crease across my face:
Illegible inscription on an ex-voto
or the betrayal in a whore's looking glass?

All those years at the Actors Studio
with Marlon Brando and Elia Kazan
are finally paying off.

Shanthi shanthi Stanislavski tatti kahan hai.

I asked two friends about it.
And they asked two friends.
And so on, and so on, and so on.

I am recovering lost particles of myself.
I knew a whole family named Richard Parker.
Voltaren Emulgel only would be good to get.

Robert Schuller's daughter is so humble.
She really knows how to talk.

Tetley is the best tea only.
More prunes. SunRype only.
Your organic ones are too tough.

Gusty emotions on wet roads on autumn nights.
White locks, lacy jags, I have dreamed of your bare feet.

Fitbit America

Fitbit America,
I am what the Wandering Jew and the Flying Dutchman,
the miraculous Peter Schlemihl,
the man without a shadow,
could have been
if only they had had the sense to stay put.

The Ernest Shackleton of the seven steps to the bathroom.
The John Franklin of the aluminum icicle tray.
My fingernails are filthy. I've got beach tar on my feet
that tread upon the treadle of the loom.
Enkidu, shunned by the animals.

Bring me two glasses, half full.
A full one is too heavy.

My blood pressure pills cause paining of the legs.
These potatoes ... are ... different.
Pass the salt.
Maybe next year Christmas dinner will be better.

Redoubts of Doubt.
Enemies of the Egotistical Sublime.
And the Unbearable Repartee of Silence.

(Setting: The Earth sways like a woman drunk on wine.)

I am a stone figure.
Vexed and puzzled in her malice.

Her hand pressed hard against her cheek-bone,
the flesh of the cheek wrinkled under the eye
as she watches the news, the devil's gateway.

These Nivea creams must have cost thousands.
They will last till I die.

Automatic reply

I can't come to the phone right now.
I am inside an event horizon
where something is becoming nothing.
Victor Laszlo is on that plane!

All of my experiences have been reduced to data points.
The whole world has been conflated into ones and zeros.
Upside down suns in dew drops clinging from the grass.
I am strapped to a gurney with wide belts.
The China-rose is all abloom and buzzing with the yellow bee.

I am naked under a paper gown.
I am the nymph Calypso on her island.
I am cleansing myself in the distant water of the beyond.

I used to sell kisses for the Milk Fund.
I haven't had white orchids since I was a debutante.

Rekha and the printer took me to see the Christmas lights.
Cough, cough, cough, cough, cough, cough … zzzzzzzzzzzzzzzzzz.
How did you enjoy the lights, Mummy?
It was dark.

(After opening all the gifts)
There was something else that I wanted,
but now I can't get it.

Shapes flit along the Kabbalistic Tree
à cause du sommeil et à cause des chats.
Violets grow from the drops of my blood.
The gates are opening to the pillar of consciousness.
The sleepers are very beautiful as they lie unclothed.
They flow hand in hand over the whole earth from east to west
as they lie unclothed.

Rekha's cooking was … nice … but … she …

If you require urgent assistance, please contact John Silence.
Skype him from your hotel room in your underwear, for all I care.

Homo faber

The palm stands on the edge of space.
I want it painted black.
Blow red ochre and black cinder over the span.

The mudras comprise a complete symbolism
in Pech-Merle rites of shamanic cave devotion.

The glass door slams.
Frau Chauchat blithely takes her seat
in the hall with seven tables.

She dabbles her fingers like the Mexican schoolgirl
who didn't exist, trapped in the rubble.
The whole nation wanted to free her.

She rolls the stone in front of the sepulchre.
Surely every man walketh in a vain shew.

Explaining the plot line of Hindi soap opera

There was this girl and then there was that girl.
But she's actually the other girl.
They're yelling at her (the first girl)
and yelling at her (the second girl)
and she looks just like her.
But it's not her.
So this is the goal of the show.
To show how two people who look the same
are the same but they're not the same.

When they dressed me up for the school play,
I was so clever and learned all the lines
and the other students started calling me Jesus.
When I wore the Kashmiri princess red velvet outfit,
all the boys were coming up to me
and the director wanted me to do more
but my father said no.
Anyway, it was God's will.
I devoted my life to my children.
I had to take whatever came.
I can hear the Lord's voice in my head.

(And the mouth of the man
who last told this story
is still warm.)

One of destiny's many pranks

At last.
Five hundred pounds a year and a room of one's own.
I just thought it would be a little bit larger.
Maybe without the Delta toilet adjustable safety bar.

Tea or coffee, whatever you're having.

(On watching you make coffee,
and hearing the percolating and smelling the brewing beans)
I'll take my tea now. Tetley, only.

Also thought the ever-retreating horizon would be optional.
The rule is, jam tomorrow and jam yesterday
but never jam today.

I do my Sunday dreaming
and all my Sunday scheming
every minute, every hour, every day.
Celebrate my lessness into a vastation
of eternity, infinity and weary oiling of castors.

They say Mrs. Proudie in #17 has had a heart attack
by the edge of her bed.

I like my Shredded Wheat broken up in a bowl
with Special K added and two tablespoons of milk,
all heated in the microwave for 30 seconds.

You'd think that they'd fix it so that people
could just sit in a car and keep warm.

The only problem is how to get from one universe to another.

You forgot the honey.

Funny business, a woman's career.
Gimme a ticket for an aeroplane.

And the muffin.

Piya Chattopadhyay and all these Indian girls on the news now

How nicely they talk.
Have you started cutting your own hair, Beti?
It ought to come with a bulb of garlic.

LinkedOut updates

What are my connections up to?
See all updates.

Saroj is now connected to the darkness visible,
a tin of Boost, that E chord at the end of *A Day in the Life*
and a cellar flooded with the muddy torrent of time,
trying to drive my blues away.

On Margate sands I can connect with nothing.

I am drawn into the core of the eddy
of the rain on pavement all night lo …

No, no. I said two glasses of water and one of orange juice.
What kind of idiot would pour two glasses of orange juice and one of
water?
Stupid, wasteful printer.

When I consider how my light is spent,
Saroj is not connected to
smart cars, smart thermostats, smartphones,
algorithm spinners, virtual-reality platforms
or how to make microwave popcorn.

I pull my walker around the Golem three times,
reciting the names of the gods backward
and the stars throw down their spears
into the realm of the anagogic
whose dwelling is the light of setting suns.

The Hour of Power
is broadcast from the lavish Crystal Cathedral
in Garden Grove, California.
How has that salamander Schuller done so well?
If you look closely,
you can see an insect leg twitching between his lips.
It is God's will only.
No one dies halfway through the last act.

Paradise is behind me now.
I can hardly write.
I am every instant hearing something which overpowers me.
And my clothes don't fit me no more.

It's Slinky, it's Slinky, it's fun for a girl and a boy

The satisfaction of appetites until annihilation
or the annihilation of appetites until satisfaction.
On the vector to sadness, is there a quantifiable difference?

They do their walkthoughs speaking about the clients
as if we were clipping collages of minimalist life.
As if we were a bricolage of yellowed text and sepia photos.
As if we were ghosts.

Anyone who makes the least bit of sense
amuses them as a sparking trouvaille.

Sometimes I want to live again
in the mid-century American suburbs of John Updike
with Slinky, it's Slinky, it's a wonderful toy.
That's what we came for but never really managed.

I do not like the place I have come from.
I do not like the place I have come to.
I, too, pass from the night.
Father, don't you see I'm burning?

Sometimes it helps to just sit and breathe.
But we keep a'comin'.
We're the people that live.
They can't wipe us out; they can't lick us.
We'll go on forever, Pa, 'cause we're the people.

(On having one's attention drawn to the bird feeder
that attracts a rich variety of West Coast birds,
including varied thrushes, flickers,
downy and hairy woodpeckers, hummingbirds,
pileated woodpeckers, juncos and red-breasted nuthatches):
You are feeding the sparrows?

I don't know what God's wish is

He is taking me down these paths.
I just wanted to be with my children.
I feel so lonely with these people here.
I feel like I am being led into paths that are so difficult.
Surely he will deliver me from the snare of the fowler.
I don't know.

The small of my back is too big, Doctor.
Everything is so difficult.
I just feel like a complete stranger here.
Just want to sleep and forget everything.
Watching and watching TV and forgetting everything.
I have to go now.
My show's about to start.

Sounds and sweet airs.
No speech nor language.
No voice is heard.

The refrigerator's compressor will kick in.
The gas jets of the furnace will click on.
And I am waiting for tonight's *Mannix* rerun.
Barnaby Jones I can take or leave.
I'm sorry, but as God is my witness,
I just can't accept Jed Clampett
as a milk-swilling private eye.

All this for so little a neck.
What does a person have to do around here to get a little service?

Consult women and do the opposite

They suffer not a woman to teach
nor to usurp authority over the man
but to be in silence.

Girls must obey their fathers,
women their husbands,
widows their sons.
On pain of death.

Burn the witch. Slap the bitch.
Lock her up. Lock her up. Lock her up.
When you're a star, they let you do it.

I miss the laughter
of my mother and her sisters
more than anything.

I am in *The Dead*.

Trump, trap, trump, trap, trump, trap, went the bridge.

I am in a foul and dark latrine
where all, but lust, is turned to dust.
Mudwoman, mudwoman under the bridge.
Today I'll brew, tomorrow bake.

Well, the Killer gonna pick me up in his 88.
Get ready, sugar now, don't be late.

Fairy chimneys

The cloud-capped tow'rs, the gorgeous palaces,
the solemn temples, the great globe itself,
yea, all which it inherit, shall dissolve.

And I can still hear my old hound dog barking,
chasing down a hoodoo there.

Leave not a rack behind.
Come, if it be nothing,
I shall not need spectacles.
These late eclipses in the sun and moon
portend no good to us.
Nothing will come of nothing.

Finally, a bathtub I can love!

Rambling randonnée through the halls of Happydale

There are no priests or rabbis in these woods.
Only the occasional miner or Wobbly lumberjack.

There are other tramps, but I am "bowling alone."
Walk along the trail looking at your feet.
Don't look about.
Fall into a trance as the ground zips by.
There are traces of animal movement from past eons.
Stories, spirits, sacred nodes, ancestral bones, prehistoric seas.
Only the old memories remain undisturbed.

These Gujaratis. They wear their scarves like this.
And their saris like this.
See, they always drink like this and eat like this.

I have eight big safety pins pinned to my top scarf.
Under that, a second pinned scarf.
Under that, a folded handkerchief pinned to the scarves.
And inside the folded handkerchief,
carefully wrapped in tissue,
a guardian angel from the Dollar Store.

These stove guards you bought me, oh no, they're not it.
These I have.
(Pause.)

You can try it for free.
You have nothing to lose.
I'm sorry, but who did you say you were again?

In my heart I kept saying: Let it be now, let it be now

For starters, I'd have to get a nice pair of red slippers
like those Turks with the fez used to sell.
And I'd still be like one of those mutilated saints in cathedrals
that ignorant archaeologists have restored,
fitting the head of one body to another.
I cannot paint what then I was.

I'm so sleepy. But when I wash, the sleep goes away.
An insignificant introit of a new day no one attends.
It appears the case is ... was not so ... unusual.

I nothing affirm,
and therefore never lieth.
When ideas fail, words take over.
Set the parapets ablaze! Fuck the patriarchy!
Take it and read, take it and read.
That kind of thing.

This one is in love with her boss.
But she is telling him to go back to his wife
with whom, you see, he has an eight-year-old girl
he doesn't know about until ...
see, they are blaming him for the paper he signed
but he was drunk and he doesn't remember.
He is a very good man
but they all think the very wicked man is the good man
and it was he who brought the paper
for him to sign when he was ...

And the pills these nurses give me don't do anything at all.

Others, I am not the first,
have willed more mischief than they durst.

'Cause if you get too close, you know I'm gone like a cool breeze

Epithets and calumny
in the openings and closings of cupboard doors.
The sliding of gluteus pink maximi
in the neighbours' tubs at night.
The 32 distinguishing marks of the godhead
and the tinnitus and borborygmi
of my own physiological insubordination.

Tomorrow we rise at dawn.
Cancel my subscription to the reality-based community.

I want six crapshooters to be my pallbearers.
Three pretty women to sing a song.

Someone has peeled the edge off the moon
with a love song in a language I don't understand.
Satan's whispers are bringing Eve disturbing dreams.
Belial counsels ignoble ease and peaceful sloth.

Help me out of bed.
I want to see the sunrise.
The earth is all before me.

(On the Indian food we brought home)
It is not worth it.
Is it Chinese?
This is why you have to go to Red Lobster only.
They have good fish only. Bake-fried.

Sleep is my lover among The Dead

Cradling a flickering cup of oil, I feel my way along the labyrinth,
breathing in synch with massive, dreaming cave bears
where the limestone world awaits an account of my exploits.

(Upon greeting the day at 4:15 p.m.)
I was remembering, the servant held our shoes so nicely
as we three girls crossed my father's creek on the way to school.

I awake to the rhythmic water drop of a tube in my nose
and Sardar cabbies tapping my phones
and sending me messages through the television
shamanic as animal paintings
or ochre imprints of ancestral hands.

Here are the empty places.
Meditate.
Clap until you kill a fruit fly.
You become naked.
Who's calling, please?

The clatter, clatter, clatter of a fork on the plate
also eclipses a reasonable argument
by your children every time.

And we went through a gate built like a ladder
and played on the see-saws and Roman bars before school.

I have taken four pills and two teas
and still I cannot get warm this morning
in my bed of crimson joy.

The mahli lived in the forest by the path so nicely.
The thoughts of others existed
only as they entered her head.

Woo me, Jack Kevorkian,
with your Morpheus Quintet.
You barber from Voznesensky Avenue
who also lets blood.

Ars amatoria

I have steeled myself in the 64 pleasures.
Singing, dancing, painting, making music on drinking glass rims,
cutting leaves into shapes, mixing perfumes,
curling lips and stamping feet,
making lines on the floor with rice-powder,
colouring the teeth and teaching mynah birds to speak.

The purusharthas of my life have been devotion, power and desire.
And of these desire, kama, is the first seed of mind.

The meek bull Nandi stands by my door beside the old photos.
Jeepers Creepers, but I was beautiful in Brownie box black and white.

Yet I cannot put a spectacularly hennaed finger
on which of the 64 variants of intercourse
corresponds to sitting in a chair or lying in a bed
in an assisted living facility with a string to pull
when my heart twists itself again
into any of the veneris figurae or modi coeundi
of *Kama, Kama, Kama, Karma chameleon.*

I got fingers on my blisters

I spent my whole life
thinking I was finally coming into my own.
Now I'm ebbing out of my own
without ever knowing what it was
I was coming into.

No hidden talents emerged.
No secret admirers.
No shameful secrets.

For comparison, the cast of *Fantasy Island*
is also now unrecognizable.

Could it be I just don't try or is it the clothes I wear?

Tell them I went into the tomb a bride.

I might be some sort of intermediate stage

My nerves are bad tonight.
My smile is just a careless yawn.
But for now, reality thinks itself in me.
I am a way for the cosmos to know itself.
It greets me like a stray dog,
ribs showing earnestly as Simone Weil's.

Ganesh, remover of obstacles, I implore thee.
Make me a moth tapping telegraphically at night
the window from which Walter Lantz projects the photons.

The moon's light is dim and its crescent pale
as the water lily the wind threatens at every moment
to tear from its stem.

This is the room of the present moment.
Its countless alveoli I weekly scrub and sweep.
Beetles with lichenous wings
detonate against the oil-lamp
and crawl broken across the floor.

Petals on a wet, black bough.

Arrey! I didn't mean to say bad things but I said something about
the Brussels sprout being overcooked and the mashed potatoes,
only, and I said it in front of the grandchildren so — that is what
she said, Beta — I was in the morning talking and laughing about
what I saw in the computer Rekha was showing me Chatterjee
House in Damoh and it was so nice and I was feeling so happy
about it in the morning I was telling the printer about all the fun

we used to have and I was so happy and my brother Sushiel used to shoot the deer there and one time he hid in the minar and the police had to find him and suddenly, Rekha thought that I didn't like anything they are bringing but I am liking it so much and the turkey was … OK and all the nice cakes and fruit and all kinds of cookies they're bringing I'm liking everything except the Brussels sprout and maybe she will get better as she cooks more but just two things I shouldn't have said and Rekha is getting upset over it and making me feel as if I am saying things now and upsetting her and I only said to Dilip I didn't want to come because of the stairs but he forced me and making me feel like, I am so sad now. And this Rekha has ruined my New Year's and maybe she will be happy this is the last time I will come here. So anyway, Kelly, how was Christmas?

May contain explicit violence, frequent coarse language, sexual activity and/or horror

I am at Dolly Oblonsky's country estate.
The philandering Stiva remains in Moscow.
Jean Valjean carries Marius down into the sewers.
I do myself up anyway for the sake of the kids.
Make funny faces like Josephine Baker
at the end of the chorus line.

You get to a point where you can't do anything.
About who you are anymore, I mean.
Elizabeth Montgomery never actually wiggled her nose.
What Meredith Baxter looks like now is unbelievable.
Steve Fonyo, for example, couldn't fill Terry Fox's shoe.

I can mug like Lionel Hampton on vibes and dentures
but I can't even be bothered to learn anybody's name anymore.
I address all the men as Daddy-o and the women as Toots.
My feet look phony as an S.S. Kresge mannequin's.

C'mon baby, give me a kiss.
Stop writing everything down.

I'm a weepy old willow.
My shadow is a jiggly Giacometti jet
from one of those little watering cans
one used to find in cemeteries,
hanging from hooks.

Broadway melody of 1984

Twenty-four Ambien and 16 Xanax.
Highlight the whole document.
Press mini-stroke.

Here, in the afterglow of day,
I keep my rendezvous beneath the blue.
Well, it's been building up in side of me for oh!
I don't know how long.
I'm not a kid.
I'm a girl.
And today is my birthday.

Oooooooh. I feel I may vomit at any time.
I need a ginger ale.

And all the while I am a vatic
travelling on a flying goat
through moonlit woods and over realms of gold and wine-dark sea.
(Standard manifestation of hypnagogic sleep disorder.)

You forgot the straw.

I'm the kind you want to flaunt and take to dinner.
I who have sat by Thebes below the wall.

Kitty Genovese runs blind in a parking lot.
Wakies already?
Stars fading but I linger on, dear.
Cool off, pilgrim. It's all over. Nobody got hurt.

One lies exhausted and ill on one's bed at 9 a.m.,
fully dressed, waiting for the ride to the three o'clock ferry.

All the thousand pieces of life's game are in my pocket.
Illegible secrets scrawled on chewing gum wrappers.

Rekha said to finish the whole bag of Cheezies
or she would throw them out.

This deaf, dumb and blind kid
sure wears a mean prayer shawl.

Hail, city of timbits, faint red roofs of mouths

It is a very silly thing to shut oneself into a wardrobe.
Poulticed intellectuals bang their fists
and importune for sleeping cars.
Make haste, you appalling gentlemen with nankeen trousers.
You noddling poppy heads, powdery anthers full of night.

A door opens and carried by the draught,
the little dancer flies like a sylph into the fire.
Come, creep under my bear's skin, the Snow Queen says.
Snip, snap, snurre, bassilure.
They flow hand in hand over the whole Earth
from east to west as they lie unclothed.

What's become of all the gold
used to hang and brush their bosoms?
Ladies will not be admitted to the stalls in hats.

How a misunderstanding over an overcooked Brussels sprout can!

(Hans Christian Andersen marks another wank in his diary: ++)

The laugh riot of two continents

I discern patterns where there aren't any.
Spirals, waves, foams, tilings, cracks, meaningful meanders.
Symmetries of rotation, reflection and whimsy.
Visual motifs from God with rolled-up instructions.
Fractal dimensions, quasicrystals, vortexes, abstruse hints
from the underlying mathematical template of the universe.

I'm a historiographer, partaker, shareholder, beholder,
panegyrist, dissenter, adherent and resolute interlocutor.
It's quite a job.

Upstage all protestations to the contrary with:
"It is good for my health."
Clatter, clatter, clatter.

A woman alone is always an object of pity or whispers.
Dr. Penfield, I can smell burnt toast!

Hook and loop

I am mired in a hiatus, a chasm, a lacuna, a rift in time.
Some kind of blank discontinuity in a unique décor
incorporating contemporary and modern design.
An unknown space inside a pocket where I have misplaced my purse.
The eighth circle of Happydale Assisted Living Retirement Residence.
Domain of panderers, seducers, flatterers, whores and poets laureate.
A desirable location for those seeking access
to nearby dining, shopping, medical centres and pharmacies.
And the views! To … you know.

I go limp on KFC thighs
and wait for a care aide to tighten snowsuit mitten cords.
We hem ruptures and gaps with Velcro brand fasteners
in a warm and inviting environment where

Facebook gives you a great opportunity to earn 98652$ at your home.
If you are some intelligent you make many more Dollars. I am also
earning many more, my relatives wondered to see how i settle my Life
in few days thank to you for this … You can also make cash i never tell
a lie you should check this I am sure you shocked to see this amazing
offer … I'm Loving it!!!

Shuffling from point A to point B

Look at me, I'm Sandra Dee.
Only there is no point B, Moondoggie.
I thought there would always be enough time.
There's no time in the present.

I stored my plan in a hidey-hole box
and always carried the key with me.

Key to my modres gate.
I fain would knokke with my staf bothe erly and late,
And seye, "Leve moder, leet me in!"

But I must have put away that key.
It's on a chain for a Zellers bathroom or something.

When the afterlife enters the room,
dignity flees through the cat flap.
The flesh is sad, alas, and I have read all the books.

Love is more thicker than forget
more thinner than recall.
Old paper that never caught fire.
So faded it could be made of smoke.
What suffers such distance just to endure?

The rippling wings of incarnadine multitudinous seas.
A ghost in marble of a girl you knew
who would have loved you in a day or two.

Battleship Potemkin

The universe was set up to show me things.
Right now, in this place,
it is so I can taste bloodless Canadian food.
Everyone else is simply a means to this end.
They have to have props and fake scenery set up
in case I decide to go left or go right, up or down,
but perforce, most of it goes unobserved.
(Especially since they hobbled me with age
and made it so difficult to get around.)
Seems wasteful, but I didn't design the system.
Who knows what they were thinking?

Last night my father came to me and held me to his chest.
I am his votive presence, like Conchita in a Picasso.
Foundress of nothing.
I hold the sacred lamp of consciousness to the Mithraic sun.

Be a dear and bring another pack of Macdonald Lassies
from my purse, will you?

Part II, chapter IX

I have entered a numinous sphere of eternal forms.
The Form of the Chair.
The Form of the Bed.
Dim the Form of the Lights.
This whole room is full of signifiers but nothing signified.
Walls of peculiar lines and haphazardly applied paint
with several layers of colour,
like the precious sentences of Proust.

I am in some kind of pantheistic trance.
Emma Bovary in the forest after being seduced.
My trip to the bathroom is a quadratic equation
through Shangri-La.

It takes me 30 seconds to hang up a housecoat
as if I were a besotted Sunwing pilot.

I have entered a sphere of pure logic where
the balance favours epiphany,
but the relationship is not commutative.
This is why I need your help
to walk across the marble-floored foyer
in fortified underwear.

I give you my warm body.
I give you power over me.
I give myself up to the cadence of the movement
that rocks in my saddle.

We're going in the Hudson.

I am wrong.
I am wrong.
I am mad to listen to you.
Only in exile can I be free.
And now I don't even remember who shot J.R.
Was it Lyle Waggoner?

Who I am, what I was, has been detonated all to Allahu Akbar in a handbasket

My face has fallen like the blasted Buddhas of Bamiyan.
Taliban gundas fire their weapons into the air.
Nine cows are slaughtered as a sacrifice
to the drone of the one-eyed mullah
fleeing on a motorbike.

The war with Muslims that I fled in India
has followed me to the basement,
where I experience light bladder leaks
when I cough, laugh or sneeze.
All the way the paper bag was on my knee.

But who are you when you're not in your box?
Dost thou think because thou art virtuous
there shall be no more cakes and ale?
You are the dream of a shadow.
You are a dance of quantum mayflies.
Apollo with his golden hair has ravaged us all.
Clytemnestra, Medea, Lady Macbeth, the lot.

The meaning of life is that it stops.
The sea is there, and who shall drain it?
Kafka was right about that much at least.
So many.
I had not thought ... oh, for Chrissakes.
McDonald's forgot to take off the pickles again.

Madam Z has corrupted Brother 12

I am as convinced as I am that I sit here before you now
that God has a plan for me always.
I have been promised this my whole life.
I have never wavered in this belief.
It's just that I will be 91 on the next go-round
and still haven't a shit show's intimation.

I went from being a brassy widow with bedroom eyes
to a rider of stairway lifts like you see on TV,
with rheumy bathroom eyes in a cocker spaniel face.
The whine and shudder of hydraulic gears,
the slow, deliberate rollout of metal grates,
parodies the iron-picket tremolo
of all the cumbrous cemetery gates in all the world.
Requiem mass in D minor (unfinished).

The attendant makes us wait at the top of the stairs
because she is afraid one of us will fall
and they will be sued by the family.

I am the little mechanical girl
followed into the clock
by the little mechanical boy
in lederhosen.

A bitumen than I am, Ganja Din

Unwrap my milk leg.
Remove the pattern of bandages with their diamond-shaped effects.
Represent my face in melted wax.

Pass your X-rays over me:
Gentle hands over sweet-scented skin.
Pause to appreciate the subcutaneous packing.
My face is puffed and cracked.
I have been soaked in a black, glassy pitch.

Dissimulate my hair loss with bundles of plaited string.
Hear my word, O Rameses, and obey.
When you're sure no one is looking, pocket an amulet.
Efface my name from the stela with a chisel.
Unroll me at dinner parties and public lectures.
Hey, stela!
Squabble with other collectors.
Pull the gold bells off my toes
and you shall have music wherever you go.

Enter through false doors beyond which
the dead sit with bread piled on their plates.
Shovel spadefuls of my body into locomotive fireboxes.
Skim off the melted oils to use as medicines and unguents.
Convert my linen into brown paper bearing these choleraic tidings.

Grind me into aphrodisiac.
Mix me with twigs and dried hummingbird.
Burn me in an incense cup: a zephyr of licorice.
Usurp my burial chamber
for a stash of slopping canopic jars.
Build traps and false passages.
Beat the soles of intruders.

Cue the muu-dancers and fellahin wailers.
I ascend from the incense gourd.
I travel across the sky in a solar ark.
Mummified crocodiles snap
arthritic jaws behind me.

To lie in cold obstruction and to rot.
This sensible warm motion to become.
A kneaded clot.

You misunderstand me all too well.
Whatever it is, I'm against it.

And that is why I won't be down for dinner today.
Just leave a plate by door Pennsylvania 6-5000.
Would anyone else like popcorn?

I started to read the 7 habits of highly effective people

But then I ran out of character ethic and switched to *The Golden Girls*.
That Blanche Devereaux. What a slut.
Did you know she had six husbands in real life?

Thoughts of a dry brain in a dry season:
Do not wish to go out.
Go back into yourself.
Get off the Paxil.

Also, the older one gets, the clearer it becomes
that this moment — the this that is — lasts forever.

After the rush, when you come back down,
the chintzy tips left behind on senior's coffee discounts
are about as lonely as money can get.

There's a lot of solace in a cigarette.

Seven habits of highly ineffective people

1) Fall out of the perambulator
when the nurse is looking the other way
here in the shed of the dead.
(Sorry, not a winner.)
2) Watch from the window the cold sea
heave and heave
with brooding hands.
(O the gulls are hoarse with their cries.)
3) Desire nothing more than to lie on warm pebbles
like a rutting, barking sea lion while noticing
that one foot of the sun steadies itself
in a ripple in a bathroom bulb.
(Due to scheduling commitments on his current tour,
Drake is unavailable to appear in this list.)
4) Routinely observe incredible things beyond Thule.
Figments of drapery on air
leap like black-tailed deer in silhouettes
over a row of carved sacred baboons
with windswept mouths
in the black burial passageways
down which the sun flames
every winter solstice
in the memory boneyard.
(Hint: Skip straight to *Three's Company* bloopers
to avoid all the aggro.)
5) Become the sun's rays made stone:
a menhir, a gnomon, a solitary standing cough.
A watcher of the dawn.
A shadow shall be your lean progeny.
(Password: Black birds die like priests in the cloaked hedge.)

(Repeat password: Black birds die like priests in the cloaked hedge.)
6) Fumble with runcible spoons in secret locks
to unlatch concealed sliding panels
to the serpent queen,
whose skull grins in an aurora borealis
set in opal gemstones and wreathed in celestial fire.
(Bother! Has anyone seen my volumizing Tata Harper cheek tint?)
7) When the radical priest comes to get you released,
for Christ's sake, pass on the cover of *Newsweek*.
(If the beer you had for breakfast wasn't bad,
have one more for dessert.)

Night work ahead. Please slow down.

I am an old woman with few memories.
My objective always has been to be as quiet as possible.
Not to worry — not to strive or struggle.
To resign myself.
To exercise my natural indifference.
To engage in a studied, wilful renunciation.
My cup runneth under.

I have done nothing that has had to be undone.
I merely judge and measure, approve and condemn.
I never will desert Mr. Micawber.

Not to have succeeded is good.
Not to have attempted is sublime.
How many can say as much?
Billions.

And I have known how to wait.
I am the messenger of fire,
of the whirlwind,
of the Day of Diminished Expectations.

Rekha sprays Febreze, liberally and enthusiastically,
each time she and the printer come to visit.
I never tire of being pushed around
by the big phone and cable companies.

Come with the holy fires

Beat the air with sticks to drive away the devil.
Rush through the village with burning torches.
Nine times around each house.
Thrice around each ladder.

Erect poles with a cross-bar.
Attach bags of rice.
Dash a monkey to the ground.
Hang its heart in a bag.

Fail to find your sewing kit after a perfunctory effort.
It's probably under a towel that smells like pee.
But which one?
Sit in your chair.
Give up.

Laugh on the bus.
Play games with the faces
in the unpeopled world.
I am the maundering centre of a poetic gnosis.
Gee, nothing shocks these Sikh cab drivers.

Grimly rue the fact that so many lower-caste Hindus
have become rice Christians.
Not that Christians should countenance a caste system.
Or that Jesus didn't have an unusually high tolerance
for perspiring poor people and fishermen.
But how can we expect people to know certain other people
come from Brahman and Kshatriya stock
if they let just anyone in with a dunk in a pool?
Not that Christians countenance castes.
Cough. Cough. I'll take a Vicks now.

Will the dead, like the old in these places, have nothing to say?

Beyond, that is, backbiting, banality, appendixes, riders,
postscripts, supplements and scrupulous addenda
to slights and squabbles locked in a windowless room
with stacks of other bureaucratic codicils
from the inapposite, immaterial era of Who Gives a Shit?
I don't know. I don't even feel a mouth on me.
Ed McMahon never did arrive
with the big gold key.
Sometimes I piss on the ground, like Eve.
Blind black worms pick at the embrasure.

Well, they killed King.
I alone have been saved.
Instruct my housekeeper to burn all the letters.

How often have I lain beneath rain on a strange roof, thinking of home

Well, that, and how one should
never buy the display model at a sex shop.
You don't want to be trapped inside with me, sunshine.
The salt doll dissolves at the bottom of the ocean.
Brahma follows Brahma.
The universes are numberless.
One sinks, followed by another.
They gave all of my stuff to the Syrian refugees.
Please do not feed the Hereweareagain Gaities.

Why does everyone think it's funny
when I say I want to have a holiday?

From what? they say.
I turn again, like Beatrice, to the eternal fount.
Stampede Wrestling on CFQC.

Now the dogs are barking and the taxi cab's parking.
A lot they can do for me.
All those moments will be lost in time,
like (coughs) tears in rain.
So here's to the golden moon.

And here's to the silver sea.
Cold and final, the imagination
shuts down its fabled summerhouse.

That Voight-Kampff test of yours.
Have you ever tried to take that test yourself?

Femunculus

I bled into the dirt.
Onset of my menses.
Descent of the goddess through the rabbit hole
and into the underworld.
Persephone trapped in a tapered glass phial.
The world is vast and idleness is happiness.

For a time, I exhibited a certain Gibson Girl panache
with just a teasing touch of Varga Girl pin-up pizzazz.
Then the impulse of desire
became a dried herb
displayed for special occasions
on a tray or pinned to some cork.
Best served with Tang.
(Oh, you'll wonder where the yellow went
when you brush your teeth
with Immanuel Kant.)

And now, no more idiotic *Stampede Wrestling*
on Saturday afternoons.
I could never tell whether
he thought it was real.
He always made the coffee in the morning.

But what am I supposed to do
with his 73,518 unused Club Z points?

Dishes fly

The boy who refused to eat his soup wastes away.
Father and Mother are beside themselves, dead.

I carry the hearts of all the dead lovers
in the pockets of capacious tiger pants.

Here come the nurses in dark glasses, the humpbacked surgeons
and the roving tailor with the giant, heedless scissors.

Can you take me back where I came from?
Can you take me back?

Fidgety Philip rocks his chair and pulls the tablecloth.
What a way for Suck-a-Thumb to get old.

I am a garment of light from the first second

Encased in a garment of light from the second second.
And so on.
A drizzling dot in a space-time diagram.
O God, I could be bounded in a nutshell,
and count myself a queen of infinite space
were it not that I have lousy cable reception.

Tied with anklets of 500 tiny bells,
my feet begin the dazzling display
of kathak, kathak, kathak,
all the way to the bathroom.

Thou sure and firm-set Earth,
hear not my steps, which way they walk, for fear
thy very stones prate of my whereabout,
and take the present horror from the time
which now suits with it.

Oscillations of planetary pass-pass
frazzle the aglets of pyjama drawstring existence.
The white cock's tail streams to the moon.

Veil after veil shall lift
but there must be veil after veil behind.

Leave me, I said. You spoil my solitude.
Solipsism is where immortality
comes to brush its teeth.

I clamour not for the right to opacity
but for the opaque itself.
Mission accomplished.

Major Strasser has been shot.

Tell me what to do

I am in an empty room
at the end of a colourless corridor
with nondescript doors.

Tiny strokes go off in my brain like a crown of bobby pins.
Dragonflies sew shut the eyes of all the wicked sisters.
I drop as precipitously as James Brown; no one throws a cloak.

A threadless way I pushed Mechanic feet.

I am a cloud of dimensionless points in pyjamas and housecoat,
drifting in a phenomenal amount of time and space.
I am in a lunatic rabblement that plods the Sinai wilderness.
Nobody from nowhere on the all-night train from Madras to Mangalore.

A vestige of creation in a remarkable, unsustainable flight from chaos.
You will hardly know who I am or what I mean.
That makes two of us.

What is essential is invisible to the eye.

Also, if happy little bluebirds fly beyond the rainbow,
why can't I even do this peshab, tense-lipped,
eyes half-closed, like a Gupta Buddha?

But I'll tell you one thing.
This so-called Bollywood dancing these girls are doing now?
It isn't dancing.
It's exercise.

Ghostly assignations at the lower nodal point

But as one approaches the end,
the mirror damn straight hogs all the zingers.

I shall be a colourless liquid
in an old medicine bottle with no scent.
An old woman sucking the juice
out of tiny silverfish legs
in a one-room flat
in one of those waterfront flophouses
that rummies hole up in
with old men on pensions
and lunatics with theories
and sailors on the beach.

I am trying to discover what no longer interests me.

With nothing in the drawers
but rusty old paper clips.

EAT ME

Dozens and dozens and dozens of elves
cast candy-striped fish flies that spill from the shelves
jars of ORANGE MARMALADE made of ourselves
creating wish wells through waggly cells
and drop through the abyss
where dipterans delve
through the hourglass needle
that marks the main line
through the lank epidermis
mining crystals of rime.
Death says: a silver tongue is among us.

Unhitching and hitching, unstinting yet stalled
prams filled with eternity bump in the halls
and the mind that surrenders remembers them all
as the foam of the multiverse washes the walls
of the vertical needle
where chimney sweeps fall
munching on seedcakes
marmoreal.
Death says: slow juice masticates all flesh.

Bursting from fissures of gelatin rope
Death hennas the hollows and hallows the smoke
to cordon the vessels with pectin and choke
off the bustle of morphine, the dying man's cloak.

Death's a wheedling beadle
whose tweedle convokes
all his dozens of elves
to dismantle the shelves
and with black gnats and mayflies
fish marmalade wells.
Death says: drip drop drip drop drop drop drop.

I don't want to

You know.
At the end.
To be worrying about someone sneaking in
and stealing cans of Ensure
from the cardboard box beside my bed.
Just another watch-wearing schnorrer under the hill.
My wallet in my purse on the institutional night table
with my health insurance card and a couple of twenties.
Water stains in the ceiling becoming Chinese shadow shows.
The ice pick in Trotsky's head congealing
in a repeated wallpaper pattern
and the harlequin face of Putin the assassin
in the decorative glass of the door.
Blind Trump plunging toward his own reflection.
I shall lie on nails like a Hindu holy man
and exhale a Craven A through the holes in my back.
"The curse is come upon me," cried
the Lady of Shalott.

Feng shui for constipation

Do I stand on one leg or?
Squat next to the Standing Stone
of some godforsaken Druidic circle on the heath?
Orient myself to the chalky arrows on Palaeolithic cave walls?
Hide my little lamp under a what did they used to say?
Bushel.

Explore purgatorial vales of smithy soul-making
and guess-my-name ontological spindleshanks.
I'm 90 and still have a whole life furled inside me.
A stillborn abyss with griffin feet.
Tornadoes wider than Africa gyrate silently on the sun.

I unfurl A&W chicken strips that aren't as good as before.
But nothing ever is.

Ariadne has dropped the thread.
Small mountain birds have eaten all the bread crumbs.

America's Deadliest School Massacres is on TV again.
I shall watch The Weather Channel for hours
but never look out the window.

Rejoice evermore.
Pray without ceasing.
In every thing give thanks.

When all one's aspirations
narrow to simply going to the bathroom,
whatever made one's life seem remotely engaging
can finally be forsaken.

One has at last reached the X on the map
that says "bulk of treasure here."
Second to the right and strain on till morning.

This is the meat safe
where Burroughs shot up with effeminate arms.
Dim white phlox creeps up the walls.

In any case, I was just pretending about all the other stuff
to fool Margaret Mead.

Where there is nothing, there is God

No ritual soot.
No garland hooks in the antechamber.
No voluptuous yakshi tree spirits or naga snake deities
to act as guardians if properly propitiated.
No narrow-waisted dancing girls
of extraordinary sensuousness
dressed only in jewels
to perform beside the lotus ponds.

There are only hungry ghosts
howling from the charnel grounds
and channel changers
somewhere under the couch
with the dust bunnies I have placed in Baggies
and tied with little silk cummerbunds.
They look behind at every step & believe it is a dream.

The coffee thermos mewls like a human.
The phone has been brought out to the pool and it rings.
Diabetes wants my gently used clothing again.

All this foofaraw around Abrahamic, monotheistic religions

If there are riders and workarounds
and schedules and amendments
and annexations and adjuncts
limiting the scope and applicability
of Thou Shalt Not Kill,
then friend, the warranty has expired.

What remains is an empty Manila envelope
sealed with a sick, white, clerical tongue.

What remains is so much doleful remonstration
of shuffling pigeons toenailing, with sometimes pink dinosaur feet
the sandstone ledges of Elysium.

But for that mark, I'm not sure about it.
I don't believe it was made by a nail after all.
It's too big, too round, for that.
I might get up, but if I got up and looked at it …

No one could beat we three sisters at ring tennis.
Open one of those little packets of Premium Plus tops
the printer has to keep sneaking from the cafeteria.
Stare wistfully and contentedly into the distance.
Ffffffffffffffffffffffffffftttttttttttt.

Address to bones with wedding rings mixed up in the dust and the gold stoppings of innumerable decayed teeth at la Grande Galerie of the Muséum national d'histoire naturelle

Fear not, for behold:
I, too, am roofed in dirty glass
supported by rusty iron ribs
and stuffed with rotted leaves,
basement-beached in some 19th-century ark
with a ghoulish payload
of battered carpet slippers
for picaresque but diminished questers,
supine Abe Vigodas
and supernumerary Olivia de Havillands,
sitting in one of the dives on Fifty-second Street.

Here, I am unsexed.
It's all a little too L.L. Bean for my taste.
(All of them had hair of gold like their mother.
The youngest one in curls.)

Give me a no-obligation quote for a walk-in bath any time.

We are in a dumbshow between floors,
only this time with walkers and wheelchairs.

Tell me, are we going to let de elevator bring us down?

I shall devote myself to meditation
on the eviternal lotus feet of Vishnu
and the vigorous sucking
of Honey Maid Graham Biscuit Wafers.

It's not a joke. Those are ropes, Tuco.
And I miss the smell of Daddy's Heet Liniment.

You can hold the skull of Descartes

at the Musée de l'Homme.
You can touch the many bell jars
holding white men's brains
and view a macabre collection
of bound feet
and desiccated genitalia
from Third World Women
among the severed heads from New Caledonia.

Scientists were particularly interested
in la Vénus Hottentote
brought from South Africa
exhibited in a cage
and prized for the protuberance
of her buttocks
and the enlarged labia minora,
the smaller inner folds of her vulva
now floating in formaldehyde.

There are no floating penises at the musée.
Wriggling and interminable, the naked tapeworm of time
held out in Forster's forceps.

Women are from Venus.
Men are from Lowe's.

Well, what did I expect?

The sun did come out tomorrow.
That's just the trouble.
What did I expect would happen when I got old?
That the Wichita lineman would still be on the line?
That the woman with the dog's eyes
would not close my eyes?
That I would finally achieve
gluteal parity with Jane Fonda?

I stand on the body of Shiva.
I am Bhavatarini, redeemer of the universe.
Some kind of ape, plunging through glass.
How can Satan cast out Satan?
Giant moths knock thoraxes and compound eyes
against the window, seeking sex on the moon.

I am a husk of exoskeleton
caught in filaments of moss,
recalling the creaking of stairs,
inflections of loved ones,
now silent.
The dead sit up and blink at me
with Maybelline eyes.

In what transports of patience
I reach the stolid bliss.
Night, sleep, death, the stars
and Happy Colon digestives.

The uncarved block professes no activity.
But still, I couldn't decide whether to bring the Birkin
or the Hermès to the dim light and the large circle of shade.

It was 10:30 in the morning and I was lying there
like the smell of raisins in a drawer.

Mindfulness, and right concentration

If you would have a thing shrink,
you must first stretch it.
If you would have a thing weakened,
you must first strengthen it.
If you would take from a thing,
you must first give to it.
If you would remove Dick York,
you must add Dick Sargent.
Did they think we wouldn't notice
all that hammering and screwing?
Hell, you could almost see the straw
still clinging to Larry Tate's starched
white shi …

I am 65 per cent water,
a lesser percentage than a cow or a tomato,
but enough to interest the dishwasher
or startle the sump pump.
Take away this cup from me.

Kabaddi kabaddi kabaddi kabaddi.

There is a thing confusedly formed

Born before heaven and earth,
silent and void,
she stands alone and does not change.

Oldest of the Old, Mistress of the two lands,
Mistress of Shelter, Mistress of Heaven,
Mistress of the House of Life,
Mistress of the word of God
goes round and does not weary.

She wears a tight, wet lungi secured by a jewelled belt
from which tassels and lengths of braid are suspended
and carefully positioned on her thighs
over diaphanous overnight
Depend® Brand adult incontinence products
that look & feel like real underwear!

Comme Madame Defarge, tricoteuse.
Laughing and cracking nuts,
straight out of Dostoyevsky.

The ensemble conveys a feeling of studied nonchalance.
Float her down the Ganges on a pallet half-submerged.
She would sooner spoon with a derelict after her sandwiches.

Another exhausted grandmother under a mango tree.
Her boomerang won't come back.
It auscultates the aurora borealis
through the amaranth scarf of Isadora Duncan
and the jiggling blancmange
of her many-parted Notness.

I generally like endings where nothing happens.
Like in Chekhov.
But this is ridiculous.
Shall we just have a cigarette on it?

We walk on air, Watson. Make notes.

Trump! Trump!
The swollen, crippled feet of old India.
I'll slip away before they're up.
They'll never see.
Slip down the dumbwaiter shaft.
Out the basement drain.
Into blue gardens through hot summer nights.
A moth among the whisperings
and the champagne and the sparks.

They identified Zelda by her slippers.
Turns out misery isn't that wild about company.
The coral extends its branches in clear water.
When the skeleton enters the flesh tent,
it flowers at every joint.

Q. What is the difference, exactly,
between an extreme solipsist
lying solipsistically in the amnesiacal night
and a body bathing in the shampoo-commercial glow
of deracinated purpose in a coffin or morgue compartment?
A. More head room.

The moon rises in the night sky.
The crab rises from its watery depths.
The girl walks in the woods.
Solitude crackles in the hearing aid.
Bones rattle under the bed.

See! sweet and sound she sleeps
between the paws
of the tender wolf.
I cover my ears.
Hear the blood flow in the capillaries.
Open myself to the resonance of the source.
AUM is the sound of the radiance of God.

There is.
There is something in my spam queue at the moment.
I believe it's me.
I'm the bearded lady who yearns to be a stenographer
and have geraniums on the sill.
I roll a cantaloupe in my hands
as if it were a planet with canals
and I, God.

Hand me down my walking cane.
I'm gonna catch that midnight train.
Like the president, my drug is myself.

Saturday night's all right for sewing

Breathing my bronzen breath
at the azury centre of time,
I am one of the lingering bad ones.
I am nodding and rocking fingering my thin hair
'cause wishin' and hopin' and thinkin' and prayin'
and plannin' and dreamin'
blow tiny bubbles in spacetime.
The cosmos opens and shuts,
accepting them among its reflections.

The waking head rubbishes out of the draggled lot.
With no particular face to show.

But if one wishes to return to the Source of Being
one always has to take the first step.
Holotropic breathwork be damned!

Fit me with a Dutch cap
in the anteroom of the afterlife.
The ultimate leave taking
is the leaving of God for God.
From going to and fro in the earth,
and from walking down in it.
Oh, the humanity.
Oh, the places you'll go.

You'll pardon me, gentlemen,
but I must get ready for my scene.
My browser is deprecated.
And then some.

When, oh when, will Dr. Phil walk hand in hand with me
at the end of this existential burlesque?
(We both, it has to be said, owe an awful lot to Oprah.)

Madness, Diana.
Virulent madness.
And the microphone smells like a beer.

Greetings to the people. This is Tanya.
And I still miss Zellers.

Where are my little purses with the coloured flowers?

They have taken these things with the hair dye inside.
That is the most important thing.
Where are my brushes? The big one and the little one.
For hair only I was using those.

They arranged my things and now I can't find anything.
Medicinal stockings on a hanger on the shower rod.
Potlis in a side drawer.
Change in many purses.
Mirrors, mirrors, mirrors and there's nothing in them.

I'm a stranger here myself at the Marriott Infinity.
A shadow, a dream, a twittering bat.
Sinister strangers hand the heroine curious messages.
Empty theatres show grotesque plays
and the hallway has a thousand identical doors.
The furniture taps out messages.
I exude sandalwood perfume at will.

Can't you find my hair colour in the little flowered bags?
And why do I keep on peeing after I've stopped peeing?
Beta, I still have to go to the bathroom.
The diaper holds it in.

Betwixt plinth and lintel

I am here at the gate to deserts of vast eternity.
Meet me tonight in Dreamland,
sighed the old ram rod, dying of strangers.
Meet me at the burning font
of the thirsty Dipper
on the arc of exeunt omnes,
hitching post of the moon.
Meet me down by the salley gardens
with little snow-white feet.
Come into the garden, Maud.
Had we but world enough and time
this coyness, lady, were no crime.
But time gnaws in the foul mouse hole
of the soul, twitching its infinite tale.
The moving finger writes.
O-U-T spells out and you are not it.
Yet.
We can still leave quivering prints on black night.
Stagger drunk as new-dropped calves.
Exit wanton as a dust of pigeons.
We've got *Archie* and *Silver Screen*.
Innocence shall sweeten our last black breath.
I'm ready to go anywhere.
I'm ready for to fade.
Box three, spool five.
Spooool. Spoooooool.
Apart from the pulling and hauling stands what I am.
Come away! Come away!
What did I find? What do I know?
That makes the silence beckon so?
Call my agent.
I know a lot of people in this town.

A life full of incident and romance

We who are obsolete,
trapped in our show dresses
with no one to unzip us
in the idling black hearses
and on the rusty iron fire escapes
of our minds,
we who smoke the dog ends
kept in old Oxo tins,
we whom the pretzels
are making thirsty,
who subscribe to a word of the day
and misplace five,
who toss bags of dirty diapers
under the bed
and sort in corners
with looking-glasses and boxwood combs,
who stitch our zigzag
bat flights to the bathroom
black on black,
blind on blind,
drizzle on drizzle,
we before whose sunglasses
the pastor used to stand
theatrically combing his hair,
importuning us to join him
on Sunday school excursions
with the children
but without our husbands
on blankets where the ants came,
we who always have time
for Tim Hortons,
who like the ants thrust and haul

the crumbs from Shiva's table
and comport ourselves with the buckling,
erupting, funhouse, protean quality
of druggy, cellulose-nitrate narratives
of little sardine men crammed into
white-knuckled adult card games
and knock down ginger,
ding dong ditch childhoods
in the wheeling,
unheard-of constellations
of our minds,
these crumbling Troys,
let us thrust our fingers,
robber girls,
into the wounds of God.

From the portal of submission, everything happens slowly

Now they've gone and removed
the circus cage bars from all the animal crackers,
but not from our famous displays of hauteur.
Where are our grasslands in which to canter?
No acacia trees can be seen in the distance.
Those thugs from PETA are never around when you need them.

Listen.
You want gender fluidity and non-binary urination?
Try turning 93.
It's like riding the indoor gondola
to some clown in a striped shirt singing *Volare*
at the goddamn Venetian Las Vegas.

I long to toss Cointreau bottles into the Thames
with Antony Armstrong-Jones,
a Welsh dwarf of "artistic" leanings.
I, Lady Jane the Ourang-Outang, trip in the balcony
as Bianca Jagger rides across the dance floor
on a white horse kissed on the mouth by Dolly Parton.

Let me glide noiselessly forth.
With the key of softness unlock the locks
— with a whisper, set open the doors O soul.
Let me be wafted.

Slight improvement in bowel condition.

Conscious of my duty to the Commonwealth,
however, I'd settle for my fucking smokes
and some unfailing support and devotion from
Group Captain (retired) Townsend.

They say the entire cast of *Are You Being Served?*
has passed and there was nothing but squabbling
on the set of *The Golden Girls.*

Will somebody at least set up the Ping Pong table?

Club des diagrammes de Venn

Our contiguous monologues cohabit
but almost never intersect,
proceeding from discrete
chambers of consciousness.
Sub rosa arias and artful caesuras
make a dumb show of the day.

We shelter in *The Decameron*
on a pilgrimage to Canterbury
in search of lost continence.
Last human tenants of these ruined walls.

We mime, gesticulate, hyperbolize
like all those burning Joans of Arc
in silent era serials.
Touch the interminable tapeworm.

A blood-soaked deity treads the winepress alone.

We are the flickering faces
of the labyrinthine fever dream
of a floating afterlife
with lamp-projector scuffs and scratches,
hourly humiliated by algorithms
of bent time, squeezed space
and existential wobble silkscreens
in half-tone Warholian pinprick holes.

Nor youth, nor age abides.
As it were an after-dinner's sleep,
dreaming on both
whilst our gross flesh sinks downward,
transforming into giant Maos and black maws.

This is the mill in which the gaunt blind horse
goes round all day. One stiff blind horse,
her every bone a-stare, stands stupefied,
however she came here.

Like the president,
we think as our mouths do.

Acedia

The sorrows of the world
mud-hook this monastery
of sleepers, shruggers,
hoodlums and ranters
trained and depantsed
in a slothful, shared inability
to make decisions.

Monks of the quotidian.
We assemble espaliered on walkers,
frameworks of lattices and stakes.
Dysphoric officials lounge (one cracks a joke)
and sentries sweat, for the day is hot.
When yellow leaves, or none, or few, do hang,
we eat methane and live in the rocks.
Our happiness is a lack of oxygen.

What, will the line stretch out to the crack of doom?

Variegated slimes form
on the walls of our accidie
as if we were a network
of underground caves.
Reticulated mycelia.
Sloshing centrifuges of bacteria
lit by one weak bulb where our DNA double sits
writing and does not look up.

The desire to be different.
The desire to be elsewhere.
How shall our souls detonate on high
and plant themselves in the cracks of the sky?

How shall we know our marvel when it comes?

Crepuscular clutter

We gather early outside closed dining room doors,
imbecilic, with empty hands and lips askew.
These chorus-girls are surely past their prime:
locks of seaweed strung on stinking stones
with dysfunctional pelvic floors.
Every Saint Theresa has her wild lament.
Baby, you're a firework whose skin,
facsimile of time, unskeins beyond the wall,
the colour of whatever lipliner Jennifer Aniston is plugging now.

Voices go shrill and the paint is wearing thin.
Graveyard-grinning gamin wanderers of an immense night,
the dead and wounded walk the cancelled streets
knock-kneed, coughing like hags, blood-shod, lame, blind
as under a green sea they plunge before me.
Pepto-abysmal, plop, plop, fizz, fizz.
The bottom of the sea is cruel.
Her undinal vast belly moonward bends.
Behold, I make all things new.

From pit to crucifix, feet chill on steps from hell.
In azure circles, widening as they dip,

dying of dry rot, ending in asylums,
tranced under trees by the eldritch light of sundown.
The flurry of the groaning dust; and what is left behind?
Only the white and moving sand that will not bear a print.

Doors open and the zebras draw the dawn across the plains,
wading knee-deep among no scarlet flowers.
No sunlight zithers our flanks with fire.
Only the godforsaken vibrato of stackable chairs
pushed and pulled on linoleum, an ecstasy of fumbling
with guaranteed extinction giving flavour to the stewed pears.
Thus the astounded clarity before death.
Death. Nothing is simpler. One is dead.

I have been alone amid the heart of many thousand mists.
The seal's wide spindrift gaze toward paradise.
Mammoth turtles climb sulphur dreams.
The lost hearing aid has absconded
with that half-squeezed tube of haemorrhoid relief.
The salmon is off but the stewed pears are to die for.

Beldam in Bedlam

I am the dweller on a temperate threshold.
A plain countryside of less and less,
unpeopled and unfeathered blue and silver,
before, behind, above.
This motionless forgetful.
And each slow dusk
a drawing-down of blinds.

I have fallen in the dreams the ever-living
breathe on the tarnished mirror
and then smooth out
with ivory hands and sigh,
silent as the sleeve-worn stone
of casement ledges
where moss has grown.
Scythes hang in the apple trees.

Our obsequies are, in a way, no enterprise.
There are wolves in the next room waiting.
Perched in the crematory lobby,
I am content in the tight hot cell of my heart
to eat dusty bread.

It can never be satisfied, the mind, never.
I will praise the Lord.
Did I ever sing? No.
Beasts claw the floor.

On Sundays they give me my bath.
Gnats toss in the shadow of a bottle.
On the slabs, a wing chipped here,

an arm there. The ragged arms,
the ragged heads and eyes.
Without will as chalky cliffs by the sea.
A drowsy cube of human dust.
Useless fragment of a wooden bowl.
It moves my very heart.

Wearing jogging pants, I titivate my painted hair.
Goodbye, goodbye!
There was so much to love, I could not love it all.

Pressed unnatural lusts on them
until they wakened screaming,
the distant speaking of the voices
I sometimes heard a moment before sleep.

Dazzle yields to a clarity.
Life parcels passages at random.
All its representatives are busy
with other clients at this time
due to the exceptionally normal business volume.

Drink your wine, laugh and applaud
while this little doomed child sits
saying goodbye to you.

The dry sound of squinting bees,
the clicks of humming birds,
stretching across a lucid space.
one day anyone died i guess
(and no one stooped to kiss her face)
There's music in the old bones yet.
I could not love it enough.

Impossible to feign

It is morning, Senlin says.
And in the morning when the light
drips through the shutters like dew,
I am watching a show
on a swiftly tilting planet
and tilt before a screen
and accidentally hit a button
and now the show is gone
and I can't get it back.

(No Gilbey's London Dry Gin
was injured in the watching of this episode.
No Jell-O spooned.)

Aristotle says there's nothing
to all this talk about the void,
yet I am confronted with it daily.
The snail-track shines on the stones.
Waves far off in a pale rose twilight
crash on a white sand shore.
Discreet protection from bladder leakage disappoints.
it's a shame I ruined my gown in the rain.

The black root cracks the walls.
A keen sparkle of frost is on the sill.
All out of doors looks darkly in at me.
The wind is in from Arcturus.
Last night I couldn't sleep.

Here are the bickerings of the inconsequential,
the chatterings of the ridiculous, the iterations
of the meaningless, the memorable insignificance
of the altered, estranged, disintegrated, lost.
Aureate exhalations from the tomb.

The silence that dreams of becoming a sound.
The sound that wants to be an uprush from the void.
I only know that summer sang in me a little while,
that in me sings no more.

I am receding.
A Platonic perhaps head
on a canvas sky
pendulous from nothing.
Insensate matter convulses sensate me.
I drink a thousand shipwrecks.

Cashmere: Now in a bathroom tissue.
A softness women notice.

To feel how swift how secretly
the shadow of the night comes on.
A quiet light, and then not even that.
And made the kites to whet their beaks
clack clack clack.

A still small voice.

And a boot in the ass to the geniuses who put
so many useless fiddling buttons on my remote.

Practise your beauty, blue girls, before it fail

Imagine me.
I shall not exist
if you do not
imagine me
sitting in a maze of old scraps of laces
snipped into curious shreds,
gold glimmering on my hands
like the glaze on a katydid-wing,
oh, subdivided by the sun.
The light coruscating
like Gieseking playing Scarlatti,
like blue girls twirling skirts on the sward.
And this is the reason we have old family photos
in a maze of ribbons and old scraps:
God is admonishing us for not appreciating
the moment we were in.
Salut, monstre!
Butter, butter everywhere.
Farewell, dear ladies,
I'm leaving Cheyenne.
It is not long since I, too, was lovelier than any of you.

Lascaux

Going to the bathroom
I pantomime a drunk woman in Romania
gesturing to an empty coat on the street.
A three-hour tour. A three-hour tour.
The king's daughter has been pricked.
Flies sleep on the wall.
Memory grows furtive.
The poetry is in the pity.
I have lost all my natural instincts.
How to hibernate.
How to hunt for food.
How to attract a mate.
Even how to move freely.
I stand in the bathroom doorway, being.
Hollowing into non-existence.
Did I miss Easter again?
Now I sit by my window and I watch the cars.
My eyes are vacant solar systems.
I will follow you into the dark
as golden-thighed Pythagoras.
We enter the cave, the womb land
from which all of the animals come.
I dance. I enter the Earth.
Down the darker and darker stairs,
where blue is darkened on blueness.
Descend on threads.
All the lotus-eating ancestors
are waiting for me there.
And there hold intercourse
with roots of trees and stones

with rivers at their source,
and disembodied bones.
I block chinks in the walls
to keep out the light of opium lamps
giving off darkness, blue darkness.
Demeter's pale lamps.
Rhoda's eyes are like those pale flowers
to which moths come in the evening.
In the blue garden,
men and girls like silkworms
among the whisperings and the champagne
and the stars.
Ten angels hang in the pale blue air
swaying like flowers
dreaming of moths that drink them
under the moon
as I return to the skin of my body,
papilionaceous as fucking Chucky.
These old p.m.s are gruesome but I often find them
gruesome. I have always lacked ardour.

Does your family know your wishes, Mrs. Singh?

"Does your family know your wishes?"
Yellow jackets congregate at the sugar tap inside my head,
vulnerable to flip-flop whacks when sipping at the cracks.
The dew upon their feet shall manifest.
Sweet berries ripen in the wilderness.

My mind is like a fading coal:
The old voice of the ocean, the bird-chatter of little rivers.
The toilet mourns and quarrels all night
and I can't get out of bed to jiggle the handle.
Though it is hidden in all things, the Self shines not forth.

What is divinity if it can come
only in silent shadows and in dreams?
The Kingdom of the Father is spread upon the Earth
and men do not see it.

Wipe away the cherubim with their flaming swords.
Recognize in the silken weavings of the aftergloom
a thousand golden lions. Kreegah bundolo!
White men come with hunt sticks.
To worship a god, you must become that god.
"Does your family know your wishes, Mrs. Singh?"

Like some girl's breathing
who dances alone
by the ocean-shore, dreaming of lovers,
any object, intensely regarded, may be a gate of access
to the incorruptible eon of gods
and the consummation of the swallow's wings.
Sacred dance is for the gods, not an audience.

At this moment, Scheherazade saw the morning appearing and, discreet, was silent.

Sunday mornin' my head is bad

A shrill caterwauling reaches that pitch
where it casts out all that is not itself.
I can scarcely credit it as my own
as it calls out for a change in the night
but no nurse comes.

I am fastened to a dying animal,
a maddened piece of liver,
awake before the sun,
everyone else withered and mummy-dead.
Agued once like me were they.
But I, like them, shall win my way.
Lastly to the bed of mould.
Where there's neither heat nor cold.

It makes so little difference, at so much more
than seventy, where one looks, one has been there before.

Still, every so often,
an orange tabby strolls across my mind
from 1947.
Or Marlon Brando from *Viva Zapata!*
For you, baby, I'll be the propofol
on that cat's eyes.

Nurse! Nurse!
The scent of apples: I am dropping off.
Making your way in the world today
takes everything you've got.

It's so wonderful to be a cat
and read the *Daily Mail*.

Take Mummy out to the sidewalk

I want to be humiliated
getting into and out of your car.
With my walker in your trunk.
Where did I put my purse?
Did I already talk about what they served today
for breakfast and how the villagers
regarded my father as a god
who cured the plague in Damoh?
From the back seat, every spirit upon Earth
seems fervourless as I,
mistress of nothing.

The lotus from my navel
drags and bounces behind
like a newlywed sendoff display
of cans and ribbons,
like an umbilical cord.
The stillborn animal envoy of an unseen power,
the sleeping god whose dream is the sleeping god
atop the lotus pounded and pummelled
to man's last dust, drains fast towards man's first slime.
I know just where the sidewalk ends.

If you wait long enough,
someone will always arrive
to topple the statues.

A-travelling along the underground,
sightless footsteps pad the floor
like dying cadences, or, the same thing

when one comes to think of it, incanted prayers.
I believe in one God, the Father Almighty,
Creator of heaven and Earth.

The Nicotine creed pours its nocturnal secret
from the haft of my skeleton gold Craven A key
in medicinal wisps: Don't go down to Fannin Street.

What remains of all that mystery?
A girl in a shabby green coat on a railway station platform?
Who put the Nembutals in Mrs. Murphy's overalls?

Statement of orthodox faith in opposition to certain heresies

No, no, no, I'm not a juvenile delinquent.
I move through experience sideways.
Like a narrow fellow in the grass.
Like a certain slant of light.
Like corpses in a charnel-house.
Leaning against the sun,
the shadows hold their breath.
A charnel-house!

I hop sideways to the wall to let a beetle pass.
The referee has had a look at his watch.
And still we play on.
At the hundredth meridian
at the hundredth meridian
at the hundredth meridian
even the sun room is a cage.

Google how to tell if someone is having a mental breakdown.
Google how to tell if that someone is me.

Was I sleeping, while the others suffered?

Graphomania

And then the wind comes, all at once, to the higher branches.
The mystic's mind is blank.
Her experience is shapeless and without object.
All aboard for night train.

She walks this ribbon of highway among human palimpsests
and broken bundles of human mirrors:
American gothic tableaux morts.
Skinny men with bare feet trot with rickshaws.
Old dolls with bundles on their heads watch the train go past.
I walk 47 miles of barbed wire.
Exit with the body.

Far below, the lovely blue veil of the woman I used to be
walks with children along a path through a tea garden.
A white crane flies over a green paddy and alights.
Radio towers in the distance.
Camphor torches for Ganesha.
My ankle bells buzz like bees.
The faceless old lady from Lhasa
reaches for the gun in her chiffonier,
shows her blue tongue
and throws herself into the orchestra pit.
Would you like sour cream on your potato, honey?

Seconal to go to sleep and Dexedrine to wake me up.
This land belongs to you and me.
Take me home. Boston, Massachusetts.
The idiot printer has brought the wrong diapers again.

Pee rolls down my leg.
Sunday morning sidewalk coming down.
Lonely rivers flow. To the sea. To the sea.

Heaven and hell are within me
and all the gods are within me
and it might not be such a bad idea if I never,
never went home again.

The cenobitic life

With a fascist face
I am stamping passports and boarding passes
to myself: An infinite crowd of men and women camping.
Each self is the denial of the desires of all the others.

I am the locus where the universe becomes self-aware.
The incense from Bangkok in the ashtray.
The salaams of the elevator men with white gloves.
The women sleeping on the steps of shops
as shapeless statues of Kali, Lakshmi, Parvati.
A chance arrangement of molecules
looking for a way to free the divine light trapped inside.

I am going down a corridor of thought
where I am losing all my words.
I believe in nothing.
I exist.

To say I am God is not pride.
It is perfect modesty.
The Atman dwells within.
Thank you, St. Jude, for prayers answered.
I knew a woman. She had a mouth like yours.
A hundred gourds from the mind of one vine.
A thousand bleeding arms of Bana whirl in the alcohol sky.
Whore of all solar systems.
The clouds, like shops, grated with accordion grilles.

Edwardian grandees cross paths
with temptresses in flapper dresses.
A regimental band sets up on the lawn.
Baby Krishna plays on his pan-flute,
dances on brass cobra heads.

Slow cows in the streets, heavy with milk.
The girls wash in the river, leaving in their wake
Buddha footprints with symbols lightly engraved inside:
Offers of rice in a chalice. Dice for divination.
A white crane starts up out of the green bushes.

I was there when the blind went down.
Dark moon, you are the kohl on my eyes
and I go to black.

Bedroom Community

And at the centre of it all
where the book store used to be
a Tim Hortons full of screwballs
and a store called Cash Money
where they lend three hundred dollars
for a twenty dollar fee
and the coffee tastes like squalor
and the timbits cop a plea
and the kangaroo will find you
when you live this close to me.

Ian Hanomansing is looking so sad

Rosemary has hired this half-Chinese, half-Indian
deferential fellow who speaks so quietly can you hear him
I can't hear him but he is looking so nice and sometimes
I just want to bleed all over Jackie like Jack did
or cavort in the pool with a fat, hairy-backed Norman Mailer
in bathing suits and snorkel masks.
Get wasted at the Capri Lounge
and be evicted from the Troubador
for heckling the Smothers Brothers.
Maybe even show up at an Ann Peebles concert
with a sanitary napkin taped to my forehead.
My son-in-law is English, but he helps me anyway.
He brought three bananas and two hand-peeling oranges
and some jam but I don't like strawberries. Still.
With a name like Smucker's, it has to be good.

I am in the background of somebody's snapshot of something

Nobody knows it's me.

Maybe the person in that photo looked up instead of down,
married a Muslim and had more successful children.
But as I sit here, brooding, my chin in my hands,
I am certain someone has been in this snapshot before me,
has surely left an imprint of her person on the cushions,
and on the arm where her hand has rested.

Sitting naked by the phone.

Another has poured the coffee
from another silver pot,
has placed the cup to her lips,
has bent down to study a photo of this photo
even as I am doing now, so afraid
that they are going to put me in the room
where the others have been taken
when the incontinence is total
and they couldn't manage another granola bar.

But whom say ye that I am?

The photos on their doors in the hallway are always taken down.
Photos of transient whites, serial marriers of louts on tractors.
Utterly ignorant, and inconceivably brutal.
Stores full of orthopaedic appliances.
Fallen thoughts of God.

To the gallery.

I will be cracks in bones
pointing all the way to the beginning of time
and the only evidence that I was ever here at all
will be a peel of yellowed Scotch Tape
that once secured this snapshot.

To the pit.

At least we'll die with harness on our front.
In the meantime, could somebody please call the super
to fix the reception?

This person cannot be reached

Let me say before we go any further that I forgive no one.
Nobody puts Baby in a corner.
I live in eternity now.
It seems like holy ground.
Holy ground.
One step from India.
On the ground her eyes are turned,
and, as she moves along,
they move along the ground.
It's a good place to stop.
No plans.
Nowhere.
I am in a cottage with a view of Popocatépetl
and the choice checkered tables at Elaine's.
Radiance is inside.
Relax, you're soaking in it.
More than just mild.
In the sink, the suds last a lifetime.
The great way is not so difficult
for those who have no preferences.
We are soul. We are infinite.
Better than fresh squeezed.
Jai Jai Sita Ram.
But you can keep the prayer beads.

A rendezvous is missed and the author sheds her tears at Grand Central Station

In this room, a Stygian Place
that is neither quite a hospital nor an asylum,
it's back to Wordsworth, really.
Tintern Abbey and the Lucy poems.
Only with compression stockings.
I'm going where the weather suits my clothes.
The Arcadian impulse so prevalent before the First World War.
The hermit's dwelling is the light of setting suns.
Islands of light are swimming through the grass.
I can't believe it's not butter.

The flitting of bats as a prevailing sense of "flayedness"
is conveyed through a densely woven garment of allusion.
The Book of Psalms, Greek myth, Shakespearean tragedy, what have
you.
As much as her children yearn to hear her retell
treasured anecdotes about their father and their childhoods,
her memory has been pared to a disjointed portrayal
of the intense emotional lives of schoolgirls
at the select Miss Edgar's and Miss Cramp's College
where the headmistress was Laura Tweedle Ramsbotham.

Rule No. 1: Never confide to a roommate
that one's mother does paid embroidery work.

Paradise by The Weather Network screen

There was a star danced.
And under that, I was born.
Even now, I could look rich and achieve sexual ecstasy
in this secret necrophilia bar where the drinks are all $10
and cadavers hang from the ceiling
in a gloomy Pernod haze.

We garrulous, outraged, baffled ghosts
frequent empty halls echoing with sonorous, defeated names.
And when, oh when, will Rona Barrett dish the dirt on us?
Surely she has had enough to say about the high-octane high jinks
of Eddie Fisher and Steve Lawrence by now.

Granted, our prose is massively self-indulgent,
untrammelled by notions of internal proportion.
To say that etc. etc. will appeal primarily to readers
of modern poetry does not mean that this is not a novel,
only that it is so good a novel that only sensibilities
trained on poetry will etc. etc.
We have completely forgotten and make no reference
to Joseph Frank's seminal essay
"Spatial Form in Modern Literature."

I am half-sick of shadows.
Don't worry about it, Beta.
You just take care of yourself.
I want my self-absorbed children to be happy.
With my eyes just slits, because of the glare.

I am not the illness.
I am not the hole inside.
I am inside the hole.
Not waving but drowning.

Friends, it's melting time.

As the authorities drive Charlotte away
she looks back at her beloved plantation.

We are sequestered and mournful junkie ghosts in far-flung pharmaceutical hazes

The newsreel of our lives has run out
but the spool keeps clattering around.
Until someone enters the room and shuts them off,
our projectors stay on like Duane Allman's Harley.
Spinning and dragging its dirge behind us.
Rocking us in the cradle of your love.
The light from your faces is blinding.
It maketh us to lie down in green pastures.
We hear the ants.

My mouth is a little dry.
From the pills.
I'm under sedation.
It calms me down.
From the pills.

Between the idea and the reality
between the motion and the act
falls the YouTube video.

We were somewhere around Barstow on the edge of the desert
when the drugs began to take hold.

What's it like to be an old bat?

Well, for one thing,
now that my ears are shot
and my eyes grow dim,
I rely on echolocation a hell of a lot more
here in the grotto of the cave-bear skulls.
In my own small way, I daily disembody
the self-dismemberment of the all-encompassing deity
who self-fragmented into the tumult of the universe.
The abomination that maketh desolate.

Yea, though I totter
in the doorjamb of the womb-chamber
of the temple of the Dollar Forty-Nine Day death,
I shall walk 1,000 miles just to shed this skin
and merge into some stone image of the deity
broken and forgotten in the sibilating sands.

I'm lit from within, Tracy.
I've got fires banked down in me.
Hearth fires and holocausts.
Put me in your pocket, Mike.

Oh, this is a happy day.
We might even leave the USA.

Sylvia, who are you?

These are supposed to induce an exaggerated sense of euphoria.
Some inducement. Some euphoria.
Ziggy played guitar and Jesus died for nothing, I suppose.

The yogini has been smeared with red vermilion.
Please allow me to introduce myself.
I am Ancestral Changing Woman,
impregnated by the rising sun.
Or possibly by a member of the New Christy Minstrels.
(Oh, what a night. Late December back in '63.)
Mother Goddess, the Absorber of All Forms.
I'm the Crown of Creation, the Heavens to Murgatroyd.

Yet in this dump, I have to do my own 'dos.
I don't know what the purpose of a pebble is.
Stare at water dripping.
See the grey rain chase the waves.
Sleep on a single bed with a crucifix on the wall.
Wear loose pants and take cold showers
at the bottom of a wishing well,
believing in six impossible things before breakfast.
I said again it was hopeless and no good going on
and they agreed. Without opening their eyes.

I can't get enough of that Sugar Crisp, Sugar Crisp, Sugar Crisp.
Feed your head.
Feed your head.
Hey, you broke my watch.

Nino Rota and Acker Bilk, you bowler-hatted titans,
I don't trust anybody that does their own hair.
I don't think it's normal.
Jim Morrison has been picked up for indecency in New Haven.
And if I can find a book of matches,
I'm going to burn this hotel down.

Volunteers of America, let's do another line.
Time to write my own f*cking story.
I am the All, the All came forth from me
and the All attained to me.
I find letters from God dropped in the street.
One should reverence the Self alone as dear.

Marcello, come here!

Non compos mentis in the sangha of the dead

The forest murmurs like a vagrant pushing his cart.
Steam arises and evanesces from the red cedar bark.
You're on your own here, Buster Brown.
No salesman will come to your door.

Bright Betsy stands in a fog of fire.
She cries and wets herself.
Mention not.

Vigil strange I keep on the field this night.
I suck lozenges and pastilles.
Such is dukkha.
Dukkha Earl.

Andy Warhol reproduces my thoughts
in a series of silkscreens,
each slightly more distorted than the last.
I have become a mass of bunion cushions
and disconnected fragments of a series of ones and zeros
that can no longer be relied upon to defecate appropriately.
Lousy human bastards.

I don't understand why they can't make a durable adult product
with elasticized double gussets around the legs
and resealable tape with a hot-melt adhesive.
I'm a human being, goddamn it.
My life has meaning.

(Göring's private railway car rumbles in the distance.)

Did you do something with my bath bucket, Beta?
I can't have a bath without it.
And just when you think it can't get worse,
you run out of cigarettes.

Why yes, I would like a bag

There is no substance to these new people I meet.
Marionettes thrown on the discard pile.
The princesses have danced their shoes to pieces.
The dwarfs are all asleep in their beds side by side.
Their existence has leaked away.
I myself have become a sort of vacancy.
A black handkerchief fluttering in a black mirror.
Five bundles of clinging.
Timorous, like Miss Peggy Lee entering the stage near the end.
A wig of auburn tresses and large tinted glasses
floating chimerically as a Chagall bride.
My hair smells like paint thinner.
All the interlocutors I cared about are dead.
Whatever hour I wake, I hear doors opening and closing.
It's all wife-swapping and witchcraft around here.
From room to room we go, hand in hand.
Trailing camphor, sweet gird of youth.

Address to the five ascetics in the deer park at Saanich

For some time now, I have been inhabiting
that frontier where eccentricities tumble into dementia.
And once you're gone you can never come back.
When you're out of the blue and into the black.
This is where the ineffable becomes all too palpably effable.
Up against the wall, motherfucker!
I am transfigured from a consumer of the present moment
into a granular participant among smudged, subtemporal particles.
I lose words in a dumbstruck epiphany
where frail deeds dance in a green bay.
Crosswalk stickmen blink red inside my head
when the moonbeams kiss the sea.
I stand in my pyjamas and watch the world go up in flames.
I wreck my stockings in some jukebox dive.
The only merchant in this store is death.
I wonder if I've been changed during the night.
I am my own Roy Cohn.

En déshabillé

Do not take your wives,
do not take your daughters,
do not take your families
to this monkey house I am in with strangers.
Everybody knows this is nowhere.
The seams are nothing at all,
stitched with foam and polyester batting.
The elevator creaks.
Oh! my creator, make me happy.
Let me feel gratitude toward you for one benefit!
Let me see that I excite the sympathy of some existing thing.
Want me to marry, settle down, get a home, write a book!

Always they are serving desserts here.
Let my epitaph be.
Karaaaaaaaa. Written. I have.
(Also, it took me four days to hitchhike from Saginaw.)
Pprrpffrppfff.
Done.
My Revello now ended.
Il n'y a pas dehors-texte.
I have had my worlde as in my time.
Everything there.
Everything on this old muck bowl.
And it seems Enrico Caruso just pinched my buttocks again.

Between the clock and the bed

The weary flâneurs from the unguided tour of this place
are nothing but Fred Astaire hat racks,
black shadows of disease and starvation,
lying confusedly in the greenish Kulturkampf.
There are as many shipwrecks as there are men.

An uncommitted, unrepentant aesthete, I'm one to talk.
You won't catch me decrying quietism as complicity.
My own life is pinched in by walls as by inverted commas.
I have no money, no resources, no hopes. No stone turned,
I am the happiest woman alive.

I would have seen more as a grape on Carmen Miranda's head.
I wear all of my jewellery at once and it's still not good enough.
And yet, in my irresolute, infinitesimal way,
I am the world itself, come to pay you a visit.
A third Testament. A pilgrimage to judgment.

I always found unexpected places for dirty clothes,
crusted dishes and overflowing ashtrays.
Wandringe by the waye in the olde dance,
I am giddy as the kicked-up heels of Nancy Reagan.

Progression d'effet

I'm doing whatever it is we imagine insects do
in the instant before the stone is lifted
and routine scurrying becomes a comical free-for-all.

The sky is always so much farther than they thought.
It cradles smoke seeping from the dead wasps' nests
and the white ash from crematoria
and smears them into exsanguinated sunsets.

I am at the centre of a private gnosis.
Lowell thought the shadow skyline was coming toward him.
Sheer nothing's what I'm singing of.

Are you ready for a brand new beat?
The revolutionary living space has been partitioned.
Bolshevik landlords reinforce the separations.
The voting has been completed. Please lock the machine.

Make your life monotonous enough
and the tiniest event becomes miraculous.
Stare long enough into the abyss
and it becomes Mrs. Kaushik Ki Paanch Bahuein.

Childhood visions of nothing in particular
for no particular reason are castratos of moon-mash, all.
I still haven't figured out whether I'm in *The Tempest*
or *The Island of Doctor Moreau.*

But what you don't remember saves you.
Beta, don't throw anything out.
Ask me things.

I need to hear the answers.

Missed call

Beta Rekha, please come soon for I am dying.
If I hesitate like a senescent shadow,
you will not imagine the shades of Homer or Lucan in Limbo.

More Tennessee Williams at the Hotel Elysée,
choking on a plastic cap for his sad, dry eyes.
He wanted to be tossed in where Hart Crane went under.
Bye bye, mon cowboy.

They stuck him in a graveyard, of course.
He was not of sound mind upon this subject.
It must have been the Sunset suite Seconal speaking.

Is incoherence a place?
For me and Agent Zigzag here of the silhouette police,
it is the only place.

To stop the wedding,
Naina has ordered a canister of laughing gas.
This should be good.

Thanks for having me.
Good night, Mrs. Calabash, wherever you are.

Ha-cha-chaa!

A place for mom

I enter labyrinths of simplicity.
I meet travellers from antique lands.
Drink from the cup of Pythagoras
and pull into the Cactus Tree Motel
to shower off the dust.

I form the light, and create darkness.
I make peace, and create evil.
Shadows of the evening
steal across the sky.

Some people get too much sun down here.
You must be careful.
I myself have taken on a tobacco hue.
See me, feel me, touch me, clean me.
Joan London: "Together we'll make the right choice."

My dentures grow ever larger as my face deflates.
A winning smile makes winners of us all.
My eyes have rust adhesions
scabbed around the wheel wells.
Before Abraham was, I am.
And my poor fool is hanged.

My mind is a damp biscuit.
I am grimace and gagging and black gums
in a toothless, muddy vesture of decay.
A cartilaginous and glutinous mass with the TV on,
transmuting into a scanty acclivity
with a cartoon speech balloon
extending as a legless trunk of ersatz granite.
Narcotic bond of the Earth.

A way a lone a last a long a loved
along the lone and level sands,
I go out walking after midnight,
out in the moonlight,
leaving one white vapour trail
across the bleak terrain.
(Blanche turns weakly, hesitantly about.)

Arrey! I need changing.
The death-god Mot appears at the window.
I open to his presence like an exit wound.

These Ritz crackers with the cheese inside are no good.
Bring me plain Ritz crackers and I will add my own cheese.

I have been withdrawn
from the possibilities of experience
like those bronze-cast reins of Greek charioteers
snapped off and smartly hanging in the air.

Even my nose has changed

It has a pointed arch and thinner walls now.
It holds the light vertically, like Notre-Dame during the fire.
It is as the tower of Lebanon which looketh toward Damascus.
Its doors shall be thrown open by one laboured breath
and everyone will rush in, to the singing of *Te Deum*.

What witchery, what pure gifts in inward seeing I have gained!
I am extinguishing craving, ignorance and delusion.
I am knowing myself and soon there will be nothing to learn.
A bridge is a place of transit and not of lounge.

I am all eyes and teeth and blanket-clutching finger wave.
I am unfailingly gracious to everyone.

I am pointlessly picking lint from the pinafore pockets of time.
If I misbehave, I shall be placed in the closet.
Lockwood's hand at the window.

Am I too late to be feted, like Foster Brooks,
at a *Dean Martin Celebrity Roast?*

Oh, to die in the back seat
of a powder blue Cadillac
like Hank Williams
on New Year's Day.

Noctilucence

I don't know who these people are.
That smiling white man seems familiar.
Is he from the church?
I told him my daughter is getting married.

The nurses talk and write and go away
and come and talk and go away and write.
I don't know what they're writing.
I don't know what they're saying.
I can't eat their food.

I'm a leaf reflecting light.
I am a water lily of lunar refraction trembling on the sea.
A silhouette in the afterglow.
I have meditated into the gloaming.
I have subdued the body.

I am in a since-deleted Tweet by one of the nurses.

I don't recognize my own children.
My bones are the rafters of a derelict house.
The water lily bears shrinking Thumbelina in her bed.

I am fettering even my shadow by the spell of this invention.
I can't find my room.
My shadow is a dead swallow in the middle of the room.

I can't remember my husband.
His beautiful wings are pulled close under my blanket.
I am sleeping just now.

All things are full of emptiness.
I shall seek no other refuge.

Curtains

I dreamed of a constant nymph unrolling with neurasthenic hands
from a cleft in the Earth folds of blue polyester
that became the hospital cubicle curtains
which, viewed from this perspective,
flat on my back in the typing pool for the Afterlife,
are recognizable semiotically
(one means semi-psychotically)
as drop cloths for the horizontal.

Behind the blue curtains, a little Dutch boy
pokes embryonically with a bit of Jackson Pollock
blood spatter on the petty-bourgeois printed matter
of my life. I am gall. I am heartburn.
My kidneys are closing.
They're taking me off the IV.

It appears something has happened in the motorcade route.
First chill, then stupor, then the letting go.
Hey I don't miss it, baby.
I got no taste for anything at all.
And yet is the God the native of these bleak rocks.

Matchbox hole in my brain.
There's money in the suitcase under the bed.
Welcome to Mandrake Falls.

Draw out the stents
and pierce the dam
that holds back the universe.

Pull the little Dutch boy fingers from the dike.
Thin wind-stalked fingers
extract the brittle edge of hospice-parlour mondanité.

Ça, ce sont des pipes.

Pedro, you take care of the horses.
I'll close the big front doors
and pull up the drawbridge after you're gone.

I forgot to give you your flower.
Goodbye. Goodbye.

Bocca Baciata

I wake to a tray over my chest with a plastic juice bottle.
Everything smells of creamed broccoli.
I drink small spurts of orange juice through a straw.

I am in a perambulator, being handed biscuits by large hands.
I have no idea who these people are.
There are signs on the wall:
What are your goals or plans for today?
You go home on?
What matters to me?
The answer squares are all blank.

Mostly, I sleep with lower dentures protruding.
I look like a cartoon dog.

Where is my husband?
He is dead, yet we played hide and seek last night
among the headstones. It's so Serpico.
Orpheus, I shall tell you that I am.
I shape! I shape!
Do not turn away from me.

Where is my purse?
Where is my makeup kit?
Why are you turning like a sleeping child?
Who will wipe the blood from my jellyfish hands?

The sonofabitch stole my watch.

I have shrunk into a gummy bear with big feet and a blank mind.
A barely trembling thing with a barely human face.
I'd recommend the CHIP Reverse Mortgage Program to anyone.

How about a dirty weekend in Winnipeg?

I need a better reason to be here than Butter Rum Life Savers

Suppose the door were to open.
Like a kissed mouth.

A puff of wind would strike the dancer.
She'd flew like a sylph,
straight into the fire with the steadfast soldier
with the heart of melted gummy bear.

All my life I cooked and ate and slept.
Here at the dead-letter office, I don't cook.
I am mouthing this world of everything
into a nothing of words in a wilderness of mirrors.
I would prefer not to.

Kissed mouths open and shut in a see-sawing peat
of corn plasters and sodden cigarette stubs.
Sometimes dead is better.

Kissed mouths superpose upon mouths hard and
friable as craters superpose on craters on the moon.
I don't want to live my life when I'm dead.

I have seen Alice at the palace gate.
I have seen the bird that was broken.
All turns to wormwood on my tongue.

Of the pretty dancer, nothing is left except her spangle
and it has burned black as coal.
The mouth that kissed has lost its savour.

Ragtime

Something came splish splash, splish splash,
up the marble staircase.
My little silken bed was ready.
We both lay down and went to sleep.
Now I am in a paper frock in the galerie des Glaces.
They said my saris stank too much for the funeral.

Marlon Brando is sleeping in Wally Cox's pyjamas again.
Cormorants roost upon guano-whitened skerries.
I who loved thee, garish day, have metamorphosed
into black Kali, dancing on my consort two feet below,
with an embalmer-fingered subsoil check mark for a mouth.

Reader, I married him.

Turn me on dead man.
Turn me on dead man.
Turn me on dead man.
Turn me on dead man.

My eyes grow lovely, dark and deep
But I have premises to sweep
Beneath the tamarack and peat
Where lichen flesh is stark and steep.

Daddy, Daddy, you bastard, I'm through.

I am held back by thick hedges of thorns.
At every word I utter, a toad springs from my mouth.
My thoughts all turn to splinters of glass.
That passes the time.
It would have passed anyway.
Fast fell the eventide.

An old, hollow tree is my dwelling place.
It is filled with shavings and little pillows for the dead.
The glowworms blaspheme as I weave my chrysalis.
I sleep in Circe's ingle.

I sit daily in the theatre of myself
making slow, halting gesticulations
under the rich, brown earth,
fretting about all the possible reasons
the war amps haven't returned my lost keys.

I struggle to read the writing on my toothbrush.
I am being reborn in stone.
My clothes will be torn and one bit after another will fall off.
The wolf will devour us all — skin, hair, and all.

Rapunzel, Rapunzel: Little sister, let me in.
I will count the tick-tock cycles of the cosmos and the ants.
To worship a god, one must become a god.

Synchronize your watches to the national time signal.
The beginning of the long dash following 10 eternities of silence
signifies exactly one ragged step of tapeworm oblivion,
pulled from nothing, trailing, like a snail, an excrement of memory.
Turbaned orbits of multiple-star systems Etch-A-Sketch in my head.
Even a dead body is right at least twice an eternity.
Seven o'clock. Eight o'clock.
That all depends on the time of year.

Witch, oh witch, what do you wear?
Black old clothes and uncombed hair.
Witch, oh witch, what do you eat?
Little green bugs and pickled pigs' feet.

I sit stoat-still on this soda stool,
waiting, like Lana Turner, to be discovered.

Medicated bears pace at the zoo.

I am my own hiding place.
I shall never reach the bottom of this coffin
with its latches and hatches and letter-mail slots.
The loose-pin butt hinges of heavenly hostelry.
Rimlocks and deadbolts and dummy-lever handles
gripped by hag hands pulling one in and all that rot
to the rabbet-and-dado joints of funeral home pews
wharfing their mortise-and-tenon jeremiads.
Dear landlord, please don't put a price on my soul.

Everybody likes sandwiches.

Nibble, nibble, gnaw,
who is nibbling at my little house?
The night is dark and I am far from home.
My little sister, let me in.
I am held back by thorns through which I cannot pass.
I do not ask to see the distant scene.
One step enough for me. Hello.
What rumbles and tumbles against my poor bones?
Tiny minuets woven inside the casket are audible.

Hayley Mills, Hayley Mills,
I have dreamed of your bare feet.

The rest of the universe excludes
precisely the content of my thoughts. Hello.
Dead Dusty Springfield floats among the red leaves
after the soothing of the waves.

To be imprison'd in the viewless waves.
Long and sluggish lines.

Hello, Beta Rekha. This is your mummy calling
just to let you know that I'm not in the washroom at all.

You had always been calling and I'm on the recliner now,
just waiting for your call. Hello. Hello, Beta Rekha?
Where are the bags I had spread out on the floor?

How can I this, my own quietus, make?

Somebody cue the maenads.
I am pixellated as Longfellow Deeds.

I lie, like a drowned sailor, on the shore of the world.

Rekha, I want to talk to Rekha.
Hello, Beta Rekha. I just wanted to ask where you put the.
I've looked everywhere and I can't.
Are you putting up Christmas decorations?

End of final message.

Hello, Beta Rekha. This is your mummy calling.
Please call as soon as you are free.
I'm in a lot of trouble now. Hello, Beta Rekha.
My golden ball has fallen into the well.
A girl runs down the street
singing Take me, yelling Take me Take

I'm lying in a burned-out basement
with the full moon

At last the slipper fits my foot

little patch of yellow wall

This is your mummy calling.

Boats from the underground

d
dr
dro
drip
drops
dragon
breathing
beard of fire
minnows of light
jaundiced ejaculates
catheter righteousness
thundering righteousness
sodden with righteousness
blood, beard of the prophet
until this Nile runs red with
baby baskets and treadless tires
the prophet's beard flows empty
a beard, interminably precipitating
where mists fog pastoral spectacles
door to the Marsh Queen's brewery
stepping heedlessly on the bread loaf
fantastic figure on a gilt-tethered screen
a lonely old grubber desperate for touch
where Pharoah's daughter swims toward
where life first gained a foothold in the tide
twit twit twit jug jug jug jug so rudely forced
a way a lone a last a loved a long the riverrun
where I will show you fear in a handful of dust
tick tock tick tock tick tock tick tock tick tock tick
where laughing peasant women go on cracking nuts

where the widening IV of the beaver extends eternally
where Virginia Woolf sinks with pebbles in her pockets
where Edith Holden drowns while gathering chestnut buds
flowing as from faucets in which pastoral heads taper to a point
Such sailboats maintain the prophet has a beard like flowing water
dripping as blue icicles white iodine drops toward the bedpan below
Some sailboats are like the nubby nibbed tips of God's editorial pencils
d
dr
dro
drip
Maine.
Norman
This is Mrs.
Hello, everybody.
you, oh, Radiant Day.
I'll wait in the car. Light I greet
like air. I'll drive you to the airport.
power of my appetite. I said I eat men
I sleep in my clothes. I am amazed at the
that bring tears to my immigrant eyes, me,
With all of the mannequins dressed in the style
Agamemnon, for instance, sleeps on a quilt of stars.
Some were mailed early for delivery before Christmas.
Some are charred photographs here at the Cockroach Café.
Some arrive with rings on their fingers or watches on wrists.
Some gutter nappers wind up here with ankles crossed oddly.
created the Life Saver? Laugh, I thought I'd. Put your clothes on.
a formal feeling comes. I met Hart Crane's father. Did you know hel
lo
los
lost things. Each day just goes so fast. I turn around it's past.
Infinity in media res is a funny old world. All litany and anaphora.

Valley of convulsions. To lie on the floor and bite the carpet.
Sun I greet you. Alexa enables me to grind my joints with dry
hair.
in my
paint
I have   Me
Theatre
Chinese
Grauman's
are doing a show. Today is always yesterday. Fixed in cement at
chimp draws first. Strike up the Vitaphone Orchestra. Jones and Barry
the
what
are
cage   Daddy
of
The bars

I am fixed in cement by the hoof-prints of Tony the Wonder Horse.
All my madness none can know.
Have they gone? I was pretending to sleep.
Cock-a-doodle-do, your pitchy girl's come back to you!
I am the picture of the princess of the Golden Dwelling
in the checkroom of a forgotten station in Madhya Pradesh.
The Christ within on bathroom gin. I rise through vapour,
wearing the crown of Mithras. Take Icarus, for instance.
A cage went in search of a bird. My prison cell — my fortress.
The world warms. The oceans rise. Habit is a great deadener.
Operator, I want to reverse the charges on this call.
What a cell party this is.
And that small model of the barren earth
which serves as paste to cover our bones.
And the dead tree gives no shelter, the cricket no relief.

And the dry stone no sound
and the book Alice's sister was reading no pictures
so let's give it a ship and what will Achilles do now
that Hector has killed Patroclus? We can wait.
Someone always topples the beanstalk that grows
right outside the kitchen window to a land high in the sky.

Here, sprig of lilac that slowly passes. I give you my coffin.
There in the fragrant pines and the cedars dusk and dim.
Another way — to see — the sun shall be turned into darkness,
and the moon into blood. Be again. All that old misery.
Once wasn't enough for you?
I shatter the grass ceiling with my beautiful uncut hair.
The restless sink in their beds, they fitfully sleep.
I have had my vision. The ghosts won't starve,
but we will perish. Duped! Deceived!
One response to the mis-ring of the night-bell
— and there's no making amends.
The labyrinth consists of a single line
which is invisible and unceasing.
I bequeath myself to the dirt to grow from the grass I love.
If you want me again, try the Zellers cosmetics counter.
Ask for Toots.

Acknowledgements

The author wishes to thank Quinn McIlhone, Shelley Banks and Katherine Sedgwick for saying kind things about early drafts of portions of this manuscript, Michael Mirolla for painstaking and spot-on editing, and Errol F. Richardson for creating a cover that nailed it immediately. This book would never have happened without indefatigable encouragement from, close reading by, valuable suggestions from and connections forged by my friend David Sherman. A moderately well-read reader will easily detect allusions, references to and outright lifting of snatches from well-loved poems, novels, magazine articles, movies, songs … whatever I happened to be reading, watching or listening to at the time. I'd like to think they have been repurposed and found second homes worthy of slumming. Others might consider the mashup, method-without-method, bric-à-brac approach a form of scattershot plagiarism. I cannot gainsay this. This book is loosely based on my late mother-in-law, Saroj, who contributed all the best lines. But it's really my own take on aging. I do not claim to know what it feels like to be a woman, an immigrant to Canada from India or a dying nonagenarian. It pivots around an idiosyncratic person I knew and loved, however exasperating she could sometimes be. The woman who has taught me more about love than anyone else ever could is Saroj's beautiful daughter, Rekha, to whom this volume is devoted.

About the Author

Earl Fowler is a recovering reporter (30 years clean) who works in what used to be known in newspaper parlance, when there was such a thing, as a rim pig or copy editor. He lives in Victoria with his beautiful wife, Rekha. *Mummyjihad* is his first book.

Printed in February 2020
by Gauvin Press,
Gatineau, Québec